MET HIS EVERY GOAL?

ALSO BY TOM CHAFFIN

*Giant's Causeway: Frederick Douglass's Irish Odyssey and the
Making of an American Visionary* (2014)

The H. L. Hunley: The Secret Hope of the Confederacy (2008)

*Sea of Gray: The Around-the-World Odyssey of the
Confederate Raider Shenandoah* (2006)

*Pathfinder: John Charles Frémont and the Course of
American Empire* (2002)

*Fatal Glory: Narciso López and the First Clandestine
U.S. War against Cuba* (1996)

Edited Historical Documents
*Correspondence of James K. Polk: Volume XII, January–
July 1847.* Editor with Michael David Cohen (2013).

MET HIS EVERY GOAL?

JAMES K. POLK
AND THE LEGENDS OF MANIFEST DESTINY

Tom Chaffin

Portions of the writings contained in this book appeared in "Mitt
Romney: The Second Coming of James K. Polk?" published on October 3,
2012, on the website of the *Atlantic* and in the introduction to *Correspondence of James K. Polk: Volume XII, January–July 1847.*

Library of Congress Cataloging-in-Publication Data

Chaffin, Tom.
 Met his every goal? : James K. Polk and the legends of Manifest Destiny /
Tom Chaffin. — First edition.

   pages cm
 Includes bibliographical references and index.

 ISBN 978-1-62190-099-3

1. Polk, James K. (James Knox), 1795-1849.

2. United States—Politics and government—1845-1849.

3. Presidents—United States—Biography.

4. Manifest Destiny.

I. Title.

E417.C47 2015

973.6'1092—dc23

[B]

                    2014024068

There are few in this day, even of those who condemn the methods of Polk, that would be willing to see his work undone.

—George Pierce Garrison, 1906

In four short years he met his every goal.

—from the song "James K. Polk" by recording artists *They Might Be Giants*

To Dan T. Carter,
mentor and friend

CONTENTS

ILLUSTRATIONS

(Following Page 24)

ACKNOWLEDGMENTS

Through road atlases, during my childhood, I became fascinated with the odometer-spinning vastness of the United States of America. Still later I became curious about the geopolitical origins of that breadth, and that interest has often animated my work as a historian.

More immediately, this book draws on research I conducted over the past five years as editor and director of the multi-volume series *Correspondence of James K. Polk,* based at the University of Tennessee, Knoxville. That ongoing project—now having published twelve volumes, just two books shy of its completion—has, in its half-century of existence, benefited from the help of many archives, libraries, historians and curators—too many to list here. Even so, I do want to thank several institutions and individuals whose help has been especially helpful, to me personally, in creating this particular book.

Sara A. Borden at the Historical Society of Pennsylvania, in Philadelphia, kindly assisted me with the George Mifflin Dallas diary. Barbara Bair of the Library of Congress, in Washington, knows her way around that wonderful institution's vast James K. Polk Papers collection, and I thank her for sharing her commensurately expansive knowledge of those documents. At the Library of Congress, I also thank Barbara Orbach Natanson, Jonathan Eaker, and Kia Campbell for help with photographs and permissions. I'm also grateful to manuscript curators at other institutions: Thomas Lannon and Susan Malsbury of the

New YorkPublic Library in Manhattan helped me to draw on the wealth of that repository's George Bancroft Papers; Elaine D. Engst of the Cornell University Library in Ithaca, New York, helped me with that institution's George Bancroft Papers; at that same repository, I also thank Cheryl M. Rowland. At the Massachusetts Historical Society in Boston, I thank Elaine Grublin for providing a copy of a Bancroft letter from that institution's James Schouler Autograph collection. I also thank the Massachusetts Historical Society for providing, from its George Bancroft Papers, a copy of yet another letter; and, from that same institution, I'm also grateful to Anna J. Clutterbuck-Cook for help with various illustrations. The Crystal Bridges Museum of American Art, in Bentonville, Arkansas; and the Margaret Herrick Library, at the Academy of Motion Picture Arts & Sciences, in Beverly Hills, California, also provided illustrations for this book; at the former, I thank Jennifer De Martino; at the latter, Janet Lorenz. For use of the exquisite daguerreotype of George Bancroft, I thank the National Portrait Gallery, of the Smithsonian Institution, in Washington, and two curators there: Deborah Sisum and Ann Shumard. For supplying several splendid illustrations owned by the James K. Polk Ancestral Home, I thank Tom Price, curator of that museum in Columbia, Tennessee; for still other courtesies, I'm grateful to the Polk Ancestral Home's director John Holtzapple. For help with still other images, I thank Kathleen Bailey of the John C. Hodges Library, at the University of Tennessee, Knoxville.

At the Polk Project, based at the University of Tennessee, Knoxville, I thank my friend and colleague Michael David Cohen. Michael is astute, hard working, and a splendid historian. He carefully read the entire book in manuscript form, caught errors, and offered compelling questions and helpful suggestions. He also alerted me to several documents that I've drawn upon in this work, including George Dallas's diary. Beyond those kindnesses, for several letters quoted herein, he helped with transcriptions of passages that were eluding my powers of decipherment.

I also thank three able young historians who, during my first months with the Polk project, were assigned to that enterprise as graduate student assistants; they welcomed me, familiarized me with the project's workings, and shared lively conversations over lunch. Those three are Will Bolt, who now teaches at Francis Marion University; Aaron Crawford, now associate editor at the Ulysses S. Grant Presidential Library at Mississippi State University; and Abbie Kowalewski, now a historian in the Office of History and Preservation of the U.S. House of Representatives. (Abby recently reminded me of an offer I made during those days: a beer to the first among us who finds evidence that the workaholic Polk had any hobbies; alas, we never did—the offer still stands.) For similarly welcoming hospitality, advice, and friendship, I also thank Tom Coens, associate editor of the Andrew Jackson Papers at the University of Tennessee, Knoxville; Tom Burns, currently professor of history and former head of the university's department of history; and Ernie Freeberg, professor of history, the department's current head, and a good friend, stretching back to our shared graduate school days.

Like any historian who explores Polk, the Mexican War and related antebellum topics in U.S history, I'm a beneficiary of the path-breaking scholarship blazed through those realms by K. Jack Bauer, Norman A. Graebner, Eugene Irving McCormac, Frederick Merk, Milo Milton Quaife, Charles Sellers, and David J. Weber. I'm also grateful to William Dusinberre, whose book on Polk's activities as a planter and slave-owner has cast fresh light on a heretofore little-known aspect of the Tennessean's life and career.

I also owe a debt of gratitude to several historians who, along with Michael Cohen, kindly read all or parts of early drafts of this work in manuscript form and offered suggestions for improving it: University of Notre Dame professor emeritus of history Walter Nugent, independent historian and Polk biographer Walt Borneman, and Berry College professor Jonathan Atkins. For other assistance, I also thank Polk scholar and Aquinas College history professor John Pinheiro and my friend Barney Schecter, historian *par excellence* of New York City.

For creating various components of this book, I'm indebted to several individuals: for its index, Margie Towery; for its map Alex Mendoza; and for the book's overall design, Stephanie Thompson. I also thank editorial assistant Emily Huckabay for her able help with all of the aforementioned tasks.

For her support and sage comments on various parts of this work, I thank my wife, Meta Larsson. Gratitude is also due to Karin Kaufman who ably copyedited the manuscript and to Scot Danforth who edited it. Scot, the director of the University of Tennessee Press, is not only a talented editor but also a gentleman of broad interests and infectious enthusiasms, with whom it has been my great pleasure to have worked in creating this book.

JAMES K. POLK CHRONOLOGY

1795
   November 2   Born in Mecklenburg County, North
                   Carolina.

1806
   Fall   Moved to Maury County, Tennessee.

1813
   July   Began study under Robert Henderson at
                   Zion Church Academy.

1816
   January   Entered University of North Carolina as
                   sophomore.

1818
   June   Graduated from University of North
                   Carolina.

   Fall   Began reading law in office of Felix
                   Grundy of Nashville.

1819
   September   Elected clerk of Tennessee Senate.

1820
   June   Admitted to the bar.

1823
   August   Elected to Tennessee House.

1824
January 1   Married Sarah Childress of Murfrees-
             boro, Tennessee.

1825
August   Elected to U.S. House.

1827
August   Reelected to U.S. House.

1829
August   Reelected to U.S. House.

1831
August   Reelected to U.S. House.

1833
August   Reelected to U.S. House.

December   Chosen to chair U.S. House Committee
             on Ways and Means.

1834
June   Defeated by John Bell for Speaker of the
             U.S. House.

1835
August   Reelected to U.S. House.

December 7   Elected Speaker of the U.S. House.

1837
August   Reelected to U.S. House.

September 4 Reelected Speaker of the U.S. House.

1839
August   Elected governor of Tennessee over
             Newton Cannon.

1840

May — Withdrew candidacy for Democratic vice presidential nomination.

1841

August — Defeated in gubernatorial election by James C. Jones.

1843

August — Defeated in gubernatorial election by James C. Jones.

November — Recommended by Tennessee Democratic State Convention to be party's 1844 vice presidential nominee.

1844

May — Nominated for presidency by Democratic National Convention.

November — Elected president of the United States over Henry Clay.

1845

March 4 — Inaugurated president of the United States, succeeding nominal Whig John Tyler.

July — Phrase "Manifest Destiny" first appears, in article by journalist John L. O'Sullivan, advocating U.S. annexation of Texas, in *The U.S. Magazine and Democratic Review*. But while the coinage is often associated with Polk's administration, no record is known to exist of his ever using the phrase.

1846

April 25   Start of Mexican War.

June 15   Signing of Oregon (Buchanan-Pakenham) Treaty.

July 30   Signed Walker Tariff bill.

August 3   Vetoed Harbors and Rivers appropriations bill of 1846.

August 6   Signed Independent Treasury bill.

September   U.S. forces capture and commence
13–14   occupation of Mexico City.

1847

October   Purchased the late Felix Grundy's home in Nashville.

December 15   Submitted reasons for not signing Harbors and Rivers bill of 1847.

1848

February 2   Signing of Treaty of Guadalupe Hidalgo, ending Mexican War.

June   Secret negotiations, opened by Polk's minister in Madrid, to offer Spain $100 million for the island of Cuba, collapse after they are reported by *New York Herald*.

1849

March 4   Zachary Taylor, a Whig, Polk's successor as president, is sworn in.

June 15   Died in Nashville, likely of cholera.

1889

The "four great measures" anecdote associated with Polk make its first known print appearance. The story is recounted in *History of the United States of America, under the Constitution,* a multi-volume series by historian James Schouler. A prominent historian of his day, Schouler identifies historian and Polk administration member George Bancroft as the source of the story. In the anecdote Polk, "at the outset" of his presidency, predicts he will accomplish four goals—the U.S. acquisition of California and some or all of the Oregon Country, a major reduction in tariffs, and the establishment of an "Independent Treasury" in which public funds may be deposited. Although Polk achieved all four objectives as president, no record created during Polk's lifetime exists of Bancroft, Polk, or any other figure recounting the story. Widely repeated by biographers and historians, however, the alleged boast soon becomes a defining anecdote of Polk's presidency.

INTRODUCTION

Preparing for publication—finding, transcribing, and annotating—the correspondence of a president whose world has faded from public memory can be a vexing enterprise. One can feel like an over-curious and too-long-lingering member of a crew that has arrived to box up papers and tend to other final business of the departed administration. As you pore over letters, immersed in the administration's day-to-day minutia, the task doesn't always feel particularly edifying. But then again, if you pay attention—if you transcribe documents accurately, if you're nosey, if you follow up on leads and try to write illuminating footnotes and generally keep things in perspective—you can perceive events in a fullness denied the president and his cabinet.

Of course, one never fully knows the thoughts that went into the writing of *any* letter composed by another. But unlike those who wrote the presidential letters, you do begin with the advantage of knowing, broadly, how things turned out. Moreover, because those other parties have long left the building, and you're alone with the letters, *all* of the letters that have survived and been located, you can—that aforementioned foreknowledge notwithstanding—also experience their administration not as the tidy procession of events it's reduced to in history books. Rather than witnessing it as a story with a fixed beginning and end, you can view the presidential tenure as its contemporaries lived it, in medias res—as an ongoing flux of successes, failures and indeterminate results, competing goals and initiatives, incessant backbiting and rivalries, contradictory impulses and frequent confusion—all barreling toward no predetermined end.

It was under those circumstances and in that spirit of inquiry that, in late 2008, I became editor and director of the multivolume series *Correspondence of James K. Polk.* Shortly after I settled into the work, I began to entertain suspicions concerning the provenance of a widely repeated anecdote concerning the eleventh U.S. president. Boiled down, the story, presented in fuller detail later in these pages, goes like this: Early in his presidency—or as president-elect, accounts differ—Polk sat down with an interlocutor and rattled off what he predicted would be the "four great measures" of his administration.

I was long familiar with the anecdote. I'd published two books that dealt peripherally with Polk, and while neither recounted the story, I assumed it to be true and to enjoy a solid provenance. Thus, as I commenced my work as editor of Polk's letters, and began to better familiarize myself with the scholarship on his presidency, I assumed that I would soon be directed by a credible book or article to a contemporary recounting of the anecdote in a document penned by Polk or one of his associates.

Though such a document may be out there, suffice it to say that, as of this writing, neither I nor Michael David Cohen, my colleague on the Polk project, have come across it. Indeed, as my casual curiosity about the anecdote grew into outright skepticism, I stumbled upon a paper trail that, for my money, offers a case study of how an anecdote of dubious origins eventually becomes enshrined as settled fact—or as what the late Norman Mailer called a "factoid." In its original coinage in 1973, that term referred not to, as its meaning has evolved in usage, a trivial piece of information, but to "facts which have no existence before appearing in a magazine or newspaper"—or, in the present relevant case, books. And as Mailer later elaborated, factoids often have a nasty habit of being "repeated for ever after. So people walk around as if it is the blooming lively fact."[1]

In many instances, this modest book draws on heretofore unpublished materials from the pens of Polk and his associates. Even so, I obviously intend herein no sustained study of Polk or his administration, or of every realm of public policy taken up by his presidency. Nor do I present within an exhaustive survey of the many scholarly works on Polk, the Mexican War, and U.S. expansionism. For students and general and readers, I do, however, hope that this work serves as a concise introduction to him and his presidency. For all readers, including specialists, I also hope to convey some of the aspects of that presidency—particularly its expansionist policies—that I find of enduring interest. Additionally, beyond the aforementioned anecdote, I also seek to correct a number of other common misconceptions about Polk frequently repeated in biographies and other studies.

More particularly, I hope that this work's attention to the "four great measures" anecdote will be of interest to *all* readers—students, general readers, and scholars. For me personally, the tracing of the origins of this spurious anecdote and the ways in which, over the decades, it has insinuated itself into history books, both scholarly and general, has been a revelation. Likewise, on a more sanguine note, it is my hope that, in this book's skeptical treatment of an oft-repeated anecdote long accepted as fact, readers will witness a case study in how historians use primary sources to explore—and in some cases, explode—received conceptions of the past.

This work draws upon numerous letters that appeared in volume 12 (January–July 1847) of the *Correspondence of James K. Polk,* published in 2013 by the University of Tennessee Press. It also expands upon the introduction I wrote for that volume. Prior to that publication, I also wrote a brief article on the anecdote and its history that appeared in 2012 on the website of *Atlantic* magazine. Reacting to the latter, a neighbor who is a professor of neuroscience emailed me. "It made me realize," she wrote, "that being a historian and being a scientist are similar—searching the literature, building a case, refuting a case."[2] Or as Mailer might have put it, in the story of George Bancroft's "great measures" anecdote, we behold how a factoid becomes, over time, the "blooming lively fact."

TRACES OF THE DARK HORSE

"I took the chair in the Senate at 12 o'clock. The President's Message was at once announced, and it's reading begun. It was insufferably long, and some of its topics, a dissertation on the American system and one on the Veto Power especially, were almost ludicrous from their being misplaced & prolix. Still the tableau of national prosperity & progress is very striking."

Vice President George M. Dallas, Dec. 5, 1848

James K. Polk was in life, and remains in historical memory, an austere figure. He never possessed the leading-man allure of the likes of Washington, Jefferson, Lincoln, the Roosevelts, Kennedy, and Reagan. He's never been auditioned for Mount Rushmore. But what Polk accomplished during his single-term presidency (1845–49) was, for good or ill, astonishing: Negotiating with Great Britain, he won for the United States today's Pacific Northwest. And waging war against Mexico, he secured U.S. title to Texas and obtained California and most of today's American Southwest. Put another way, Polk gave his nation its modern coast-to-coast breadth, thus rendering it truly a continental nation-state. And that status, as a continental nation-state has shaped—and to this day, shapes—much of America's role as a world power. Journalist Robert D. Kaplan, a scholar of the ways in which geography shapes world history, accords to America's continental breadth a determinative role in shaping much of its modern history.

> It is geography that has helped sustain America's prosperity and which may be ultimately responsible for America's pan-humanistic altruism. . . . The militarism and pragmatism of continental Europe through the mid-twentieth century, to which the Americans always felt superior, was the result of geography, not character. Competing states and empires adjoined one another on a crowded continent. European nations could never withdraw across an ocean in the event of a military miscalculation. . . . It wasn't only two oceans that gave Americans the luxury of their idealism, it was also that these two oceans gave America direct access to the two principal arteries of politics and commerce in the world: Europe across the Atlantic and East Asia across the Pacific, with the riches of the American continent lying between them.[1]

Arguably, more than any other individual in American history, James K. Polk bears responsibility for shaping the boundaries of the continental United States—and thus creating the geographical circumstances that enabled its later emergence as a world power. By now, those American boundaries have become so familiar, so accepted, so enshrined on maps, that it's difficult to imagine a time when they were still in flux, subject to fierce debates, and lacking the universal acceptance they now enjoy.

Even so, in their day, President Polk's territorial initiatives triggered corrosive exchanges. When he began his presidency, the vast Oregon Country—reaching from today's state of Oregon north into today's British Columbia—had been, since 1818, under "joint occupation" by the United States and the United Kingdom.[2] Texas, at the time Polk assumed office, was still claimed by Mexico, as was Mexico's departments of California—called Alta California by Mexican officials—and New Mexico, the latter a vaguely defined realm that included all of today's state of New Mexico and much of the rest of the Lower 48's Southwest.[3] In four years, Polk, through negotiations with the United Kingdom, acquired sole title to the southern half of the Oregon Country; and through war with Mexico, he secured U.S. title to Texas, California, and the vast province of New Mexico.

An irony, however, generally unremarked upon, then and now, attended those acquisitions and the waning of debates over Polk's attainment of them. Over the coming years, as the new boundaries found their way onto maps, controversies over how they came to be and where they ran evaporated like water in the Death Valley sink.

Thirteen years after Polk's actions, the United States fought a civil war over how to fill the new lands and, more broadly, over slavery's future throughout the nation. But during Polk's day and since, no American politician, liberal or conservative, with serious hopes of winning an election, has suggested returning California and New Mexico to Mexico or the southern portion of the Oregon Country—modern America's Pacific Northwest—to the United Kingdom. As historian George Pierce Garrison observed in

1906, half a century after Polk left the presidency, "There are few in this day, even of those who condemn the methods of Polk, that would be willing to see his work undone."[4]

Then again, while debates over the breadth of Polk's acquisitions died long ago, disputes that surrounded other aspects of his presidency never entirely disappeared; perhaps, due to recent tribulations, they have even gained renewed force. In legacy if not in name, Polk still weighs upon us. By the terms of the 1848 Treaty of Guadalupe Hidalgo, which concluded the Mexican War, California and other western realms became U.S. territory; and Mexican citizens living in the annexed lands who chose to remain within those realms were guaranteed the full rights of U.S. citizenship. Against that background, the response of public officials, in 1998, to the sesquicentennial of the Treaty of Guadalupe Hidalgo underscored the still combustible properties of the treaty's—and by implication Polk's—legacies.

Public officials on both sides of the Mason-Dixon line routinely, and often boisterously, mark anniversaries associated with the American Civil War. But as 1998 approached, officials in California, New Mexico, and other western climes that had entered the Union as part of the 1848 Mexican Cession deemed the treaty—and by implication Polk's legacy—too divisive for public celebration. For the most part, they let the anniversary pass without fanfare.

In March 1998, weeks after that sesquicentennial, *Los Angeles Times* columnist Frank del Olmo noted the silence, official and otherwise, that had attended the treaty's anniversary. He also described the pact's often troublesome legacy. "Its echoes are heard in debates over everything from illegal immigration to NAFTA to which national team Mexican-born soccer fans in Los Angeles should root for." Del Olmo also noted the treaty's frequent invocation by Latino activists who use it to argue for claimed rights to bilingual education and other cultural programs. Many such cases, he believed, rested on "shaky ground." But another ramification of the treaty was, to his mind, beyond dispute: it "created the first generation of Mexican Americans by guaranteeing the Mexicans who inhabited the ceded territories the right to their property, language and culture."

Given all that, del Olmo found it "odd that people in this country are taking note of the centennial of the outbreak of the Spanish-American War—the sinking the battleship Maine was on Feb. 15, 1898—while at the same time virtually ignoring an important anniversary in the Mexican-American War." The Treaty of Guadalupe Hidalgo, he pointed out, had "ended hostilities in a much longer" conflict than the Spanish-American War."[5]

Still more recently, as this is written in the early twenty-first century, echoes of Polk-era debates also resonate in contemporary conversations concerning the propriety of American foreign wars that lead to troublesome occupations; and, more broadly, the growing pains of a federal union that, forsaking its Anglo-Saxon self-image of Polk's era, increasingly acknowledges a wide range of ethnic identities.

Born in North Carolina in 1795, James K. Polk moved with his family to Tennessee while he was still a boy. There, in the town of Columbia, growing up as the son of a prosperous farmer and judge, the future president spent his formative years. Beginning in 1813, he studied for two years at private academies near Columbia before leaving for the University of North Carolina in Chapel Hill. There Polk's studies included mathematics, classical literature and languages, and natural and moral philosophy.[6]

After graduating in 1818, Polk returned to Columbia, where he began successful careers as a trial lawyer and in politics. In 1824, he married Sarah Childress, the refined daughter of a prosperous Tennessee planter and businessman. Polk eventually became a protégé of fellow Tennessean Andrew Jackson—and was thus dubbed "Young Hickory" in reference to his relationship with "Old Hickory." He rose quickly in state and federal politics. Between 1823 and his death in 1849, Polk served as a member of the state legislature (1823–25) and the U.S. House of Representatives (1825–39), as chairman of the latter body's Ways and Means Committee (1833–35), as its Speaker (1835–39), and as governor of Tennessee (1839–41).

In 1841 and 1843, Polk lost races for the Tennessee governorship. With his political career stalled, allies in 1844 began exploring ways to elevate him to the number-two spot on that year's Democratic presidential ticket. As the national convention approached, former president Martin Van Buren seemed the party's likely presidential nominee. But when Van Buren's opponents implemented a rule that required the nominee to muster a two-thirds majority of the delegates, his chances faded. In the wake of his candidacy's collapse and, successively, that of several others, the convention faced a deadlock. Not until its ninth ballot was the nominee, James K. Polk, chosen.

With allies in both the North and South, the Tennessean had emerged as the compromise candidate. (The vice presidential nomination, originally envisioned for Polk by his supporters, went instead to former Philadelphia mayor and U.S. senator from Pennsylvania George M. Dallas.) Polk's triumph as the party's presidential nominee was an unexpected feat, one widely believed to have occasioned the first usage in presidential politics of the term "dark horse." In the November election, Polk narrowly defeated the Whig party nominee, Kentuckian Henry Clay. In the popular vote, Polk beat Clay by less than 2 percent; in the electoral college, he won by a margin of 170 to 105.[7] In March 1845, when Polk took the oath of office, he was, at forty-nine, the youngest man to have assumed the presidency.

Among the events that defined Polk's years as president, none carried more urgency than those concerning the Mexican War.[8] Between May 1846 and July 1847, the president's supporters thrilled as names such as Palo Alto, Resaca del Palma, Santa Fe, Monterey (California), Monterrey (in Mexico's east), Buena Vista, Sacramento (in Chihuahua, Mexico), Veracruz, and Cerro Gordo, trumpeted by the era's penny press, became landmarks of the triumph of American forces.[9]

In July 1847, the conflict's final engagements—culminating in the capture in September of Mexico City[10]—lay more than two months away. So already, by that July, heedless of Whig critics, the administration and its allies were busy pondering the war's territorial spoils for the United States.[11]

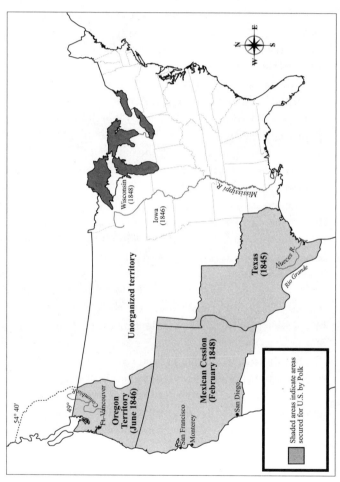

"The United States, February 1848, The Legacy of James K. Polk"

THE EXPANSIONIST

The fuse that ignited the United States' war with Mexico was lit by Polk's predecessor, John Tyler. On February 28, 1845, four days before Polk took office, Congress, at President Tyler's behest, passed a joint resolution extending the Republic of Texas a long-sought invitation to apply for U.S. annexation. Predictably, Mexican officials condemned Congress' action. They disputed the border claimed by Texas; that republic expansively claimed all land north and east of the Rio Grande, whereas Mexico regarded the more northerly Nueces River as Texas' boundary. Raising tensions still higher, Mexico had never officially recognized Texas' independence—and had vowed that annexation of the contested realm would be regarded as a belligerent act against Mexico.

Disregarding those concerns, Texas, on December 29, 1845—at least in the eyes of officials in Austin and Washington—was formally accorded U.S. statehood. Weeks earlier, in his first annual message to Congress, Polk, wary of European interference in the annexation of Texas, had reached back to President James Monroe's seventh annual message to Congress (1823). Quoting Monroe, Polk—presenting U.S. expansionism in anticolonial language—declared, "The American continents . . . are henceforth not to be considered as subjects for future colonization by any European powers." That fall Polk applied to Monroe's admonition the term by which, shorn of the honorific and its possessive form, it has henceforth been known: "Mr. Monroe's doctrine."[1]

Four months later, in April 1846, came an attack on U.S. soldiers by Mexican troops near the mouth of the Rio Grande, in the disputed border region between Texas and Mexico. In May, Congress, at Polk's behest, declared war on Mexico. The president's enemies—antiwar Whigs and Democrats, abolitionists, and assorted opponents of the spread of slavery—were outraged. Three months later, and repeatedly over the next two years, Pennsylvania congressman David Wilmot, a Democrat, and other members of Congress introduced legislation to ban slavery in any territory won through the war. The measure, soon called the Wilmot Proviso, passed the House several times but never won Senate approval. Much of the support for the Wilmot Proviso, however, arose less from principled opposition to slavery and more from a desire to preserve labor opportunities for white settlers in any new lands won during the war. Wilmot himself accepted a term supporters coined for the measure; they called it a "White Man's Proviso."[2]

Echoing the outrage of other Americans who opposed the Mexican War on moral grounds, abolitionist Frederick Douglass, lecturing in England in September 1846, assayed the morality of a war against a republic that upon its founding in 1821 had outlawed slavery. He condemned the United States for "now seeking to perpetuate and extend the conquests of slavery, and waging a bloody war with Mexico that she may establish slavery on a soil where a semi-barbarous people had the humanity to put an end to it."[3]

For President Polk and his cabinet, however, the war declaration of May 1846 had marked a heady moment. The administration at that time was close to concluding negotiations that would extend Old Glory's dominion to the Pacific Coast. In June 1846, a treaty negotiated by Secretary of State James Buchanan and British minister Sir Richard Pakenham resolved long-simmering geopolitical rivalries between the United States and the United Kingdom over the sprawling Oregon Country. By the pact's terms, Britain retained title to the area now occupied by Canada's province of British Columbia, and Uncle Sam acquired exclusive title to a domain that included all of the area occupied by today's states of Washington, Oregon, and Idaho and the western portions of Montana and Wyoming. Put another way, the two countries agreed to divide the Oregon Country along the forty-ninth parallel, which forms most of the western stretch of today's U.S.-Canadian border.

Emboldened by that outcome, Polk and his supporters, seizing on the April 1846 military clash near the mouth of the Rio Grande but acting on an earlier-contemplated option, settled on war with Mexico as a means by which the United States might secure its claim on Texas and, as policy objectives evolved, the entirety of Mexico's sparsely settled northwestern frontier. That frontier included Mexico's departments of New Mexico and California. Eventually, in February 1848, by the Treaty of Guadalupe Hidalgo between the United States and Mexico, the president secured all of those lands.[4]

In March 1847, looking back on those triumphs, Polk stood at the chronological halfway mark of his four-year presidential term. Most first-term presidents facing that milestone would have been preoccupied with reelection strategies. But not the fifty-one-year-old Tennessean. As a candidate, Polk—matching a promise made by his Whig opponent Clay—had forsworn a second term; if elected, he had promised, his turn in the White House would be for four years, and four years only.

Thus, from one perspective, the new president had begun his administration already a lame duck. In March 1845, when Polk took office, friends, enemies, and rivals alike—Democrats and Whigs—knew, barring unforeseen events, exactly how many days remained in his presidency. Accordingly, as the days passed, they could gage with precision his ostensibly declining powers to reward or punish. But from another vantage, candidate Polk's no-second-term promise gave President Polk a singular advantage: having no need to go back to voters to win a second term, he was free to pursue his policies unburdened by the circumspections that inhibit a president who knows he must again face the electorate.

A glass half full or half empty?

The metaphor ill suits a man of such abstemious habits. Nonetheless, Polk and his cabinet viewed his presidency, at its midpoint, as a half-full glass. That spirit of exaltation propels a letter he wrote in January 1847 to George Bancroft, his ambassador to the Court of St. James:

> For myself, I rejoice that I am under no circumstances to be before the Country for re-election. This

determination is irrevocable. Personally—therefore I have no interest, in the question of the succession, but I most ardently desire to maintain the ascendancy of my political principles, and to hand over the Government, at the close of my term, to a successor of my own political faith.[5]

In words and actions, Polk seems to have been emboldened, not hindered, by his one-term pledge. Indeed, if anything, as the missive to Bancroft suggests, the promise added an urgency—and vigor—to his ever-dwindling days in office. Beyond that, the entire body of his correspondence and presidential diary indicate no wavering on his one-term pledge.

Then and now, Polk's diplomatic achievement in Oregon and his military successes in Mexico, actions that won plaudits from leaders both domestic and foreign, have placed an aura of invincibility over his presidency. Conventional wisdom associates that presidency, indeed Polk's very name, with "Manifest Destiny," a locution coined in 1845 by journalist John L. O'Sullivan. Writing in *The United States Magazine and Democratic Review,* a literary and political journal that he co-owned, O'Sullivan, while calling for U.S. annexation of Texas, argued that it is "our manifest destiny to overspread the continent allotted by Providence for the free development of our yearly multiplying millions."[6]

Soon popularized by the era's penny press, the term never received a precise definition. A Procrustean phrase, more often invoked in its day by those selling newspapers than by policymakers, it came to refer to an unbridled, in most cases east-to-west, U.S. expansionism ordained by a Protestant, Anglo-Saxon God. That most of the lands eyed for conquest were home to native peoples and other non-Anglo-Saxon populations mattered little to Manifest Destiny's adherents. Nor, for that matter, did U.S. settlers always proceed from east to west. Often, as with those Texas-bound, many moved from northeast to southwest; in California, with many arrivals coming via the Pacific, newcomers often moved from west to east.

Polk achieved most but not all of the expansionist projects sought by Manifest Destiny's advocates. As a candidate, he had run on a party platform that pledged to fight for a northern U.S. border in the Oregon County, which stretched deep into today's British Columbia. "Fifty-four Forty or Fight," the trademark phrase associated with that advocacy—though often linked to Polk's campaign—did not come into use until a year into his term.[7] Those—known as Oregon "ultras"—who invoked the phrase were thus crestfallen when, as president, Polk agreed to the Buchanan-Pakenham treaty that established a border between the two coutnries at the 49th Parallel, except where it dipped south to accord the United Kingdom title to all of Vamcouver Island. Extending the 49th Parallel border established by earlier treaties, it was the same line that today, stretching westward from Lake of the Woods, Minnesota, demarcates, in those realms, the U.S.–Canada border.

U.S. expansionists who favored acquisition of the entirety of Mexico and the island of Cuba were similarly disappointed. As the war in Mexico neared its end, much of the nation's expansionist penny press—papers such as the *Boston Times* and the *New York Sun*—called for Polk, when negotiating an armistice, to acquire all of Mexico. In 1848, however, the administration—wary of the burdens that such an occupation of the entirety of Mexico would entail—accepted a more modest territorial settlement.

Likewise, the president disappointed supporters of American annexation of Cuba. The idea of U.S. acquisition of Cuba enjoyed a long pedigree in American politics—stretching back to such early advocates as Presidents Thomas Jefferson, James Madison, and James Monroe.[8] During Polk's term in office, invigorated by recent expansionist triumphs, the cause won a new cadre of advocates, whose numbers included South Carolina U.S. senator John C. Calhoun, secretary of state James Buchanan, and journalist and Democratic party activist John O'Sullivan.

Indeed, on May 10, 1848, during the administration's waning months, Polk met with O'Sullivan and Illinois senator Stephen Douglas to discuss the island. The two hoped to persuade the president to support an audacious scheme proposed by the Club de la Habana, a cabal of wealthy Cuban entrepreneurs and planters.

The government of Spain, Cuba's colonial overseer, was heavily indebted to the United Kingdom, and the well-healed Cubans feared that Madrid might, in exchange for London's forgiving of those debts, yield to pressures from British abolitionists and abolish slavery on the island. Thus the Club de la Habana, via O'Sullivan and Douglas, extended a proposal to the president: If Polk would oversee a U.S. purchase of Cuba from Spain, the Cubans would reimburse the U.S. Treasury up to one hundred million dollars.

Polk heard out Douglas and O'Sullivan, but the two left the White House with no inkling of the president's reaction to their proposal. As it happened, the often inscrutable president had already, weeks earlier, made up his mind on Cuba. As Polk confided to his diary mere hours after his meeting with O'Sullivan and Buchanan, "Though I expressed no opinion to them I am decidedly in favor of purchasing Cuba & making it one of the States of [the] Union."

Weeks later, in June 1848, Polk ordered Secretary of State Buchanan to authorize Romulus Saunders, the U.S. minister in Madrid, to offer Spain up to one hundred million dollars for the island. In his instructions to Saunders, Buchanan advised the envoy to, while making the offer, "touch delicately upon the dangers that Spain may lose Cuba by revolution in the Island, or that it might be wrested from her by Great Britain." In the end, however, diplomatic ineptitude by Saunders, combined with reporting by the *New York Herald* on the ostensibly secret overture, embarrassed Spanish officials and the talks were abruptly ended.[9]

In the end, of course, disappointments notwithstanding, Polk did win more than his share of expansionist triumphs. And those victories won wide approval among his supporters. Beyond that, the nation's new status as a continental nation-state soon became enshrined in its self-image—and was celebrated, in often florid language, by its politicians and writers; "I skirt the sierras," rhapsodized Walt Whitman, "my palms cover continents." Henry David Thoreau famously refused to pay a tax because of his opposition to the war, an act that landed him in jail. But over time, poetically if not politically, even the bard of Walden Pond could not resist the spell: "Eastward I go only by force," Thoreau eventually wrote, "but westward I go free."[10]

Indeed, for good or ill, in a broader if poetic sense Polk, Frémont and others of that generation—in their extension of the nation's domain, bequeathing to America its coast-to-coast breadth—gave the country's artists a continental template on which to work, the open road down which American writers, from Jack Kerouac to Robert Pirsig, Mark Twain to Hunter Thompson, John Steinbeck to Woody Guthrie have traveled. Literally and metaphorically, Route 66 runs deep into 1848 Mexican Cession country.

His public aversion to sentimentality notwithstanding, Polk's writings do reveal a gentle side to the president. Letters to family members and those penned as he conducted a brief sentimental journey in May 1847 to his alma mater, the University of North Carolina in Chapel Hill, evoke a softer, even solicitous, side to his personality. However heavily the duties of office occupied his time, family and friends remained important to him. Of the North Carolina visit's first day, he recorded in his diary, "I have never spent a more pleasant or delightful afternoon & evening."[11]

By the time Polk became president, his mane of once-black hair had faded to gray. Of medium height with a high forehead and a prominent nose, he was an introvert who adapted to the demands of the two professions, trial lawyer and politician, which became his life work. Much like President Richard Nixon, Polk was an introvert in an extrovert's profession.

An assertion, widely repeated by Polk biographers, describes his acumen for public speaking as winning him the accolade "Napoleon of the Stump." But no usage of that sobriquet during Polk's lifetime has been located. Indeed, its earliest located appearance occurs in John S. Jenkins's *Life of James Knox Polk: Late President of the United States,* published in 1850.[12]

Suffice it to say, then, that Polk was not a glad-hander. When he could, particularly as president, he often avoided public events and declined invitations. But when necessity called, he could and did rise to the occasion. After all, he did enjoy success in *both* of his chosen occupations. And as leader of the nation, Polk set aside two evenings each week during which citizens could visit the White House and air concerns to their president.[13]

Tempering his often dour image, contemporary correspondence and accounts of the Polks' life in Washington reveal, by Victorian standards, a tender and equable relationship between him and his wife, Sarah Polk. An able woman, Sarah possessed an advanced education and formidable intelligence. Her counsel, in business and politics, was often sought by her husband. The Polks had no children, but the portrait of their White House life that emerges in the letters is further softened by the retinue of nieces and nephews from Tennessee who stayed for extended visits.[14]

Even so, in most cases, in words and deeds, Polk presented a coldly formal, no-nonsense persona to the world. And that approach, more than sentimental interludes with family and college memories, precluded his adoption of the western fervor of John O'Sullivan and other contemporaries. In fact, so far as we know, Polk never uttered or penned the phrase "Manifest Destiny." Not for this pragmatic politician the bombastic rhetoric that issued from such a gaseous notion. Indeed, Thomas Hart Benton, in his memoirs, published in 1883, insisted that the man whose name is linked to the Mexican War was enamored neither of war—at least for its own sake—nor of romantic nationalism:

It is impossible to conceive of an administration less warlike, or more intriguing, that that of Mr. Polk. They were men of peace, with objects to be accomplished by means of war; so that war was a necessity and an indispensability to their purpose; but they wanted no more of it than would answer their purposes. They wanted a small war, just large enough to require a treaty of peace, and not large enough to make military reputations, dangerous for the presidency. Never were men at the head of a government less imbued with military spirit, or more addicted to intrigue.[15]

More to the point, each expansionist project Polk undertook was designed to appeal to specific constituencies—Texas to southern planters and aspirant pioneers from that region; Oregon and California to, among others, mid-Atlantic and New England commercial and maritime interests, as well as aspirant emigrants from that day's "Northwest," today's Midwest.

Privately and publicly, however naively in retrospect, Polk always insisted that whether acquired territories permitted or banned slavery was a separate issue, subordinate to the national interest of expanding the nation's geographic breadth and furthering "the Union." An August 10, 1846, diary entry bears witness to that attitude.

The entry concerns the Wilmot Proviso, adopted days earlier by the House of Representatives, which sought to ban slavery in any territory acquired from Mexico. Polk dismisses the amendment as "mischievous & foolish": "What connection slavery had with making peace with Mexico it is difficult to conceive."

Eight months later, he was equally dismissive toward efforts to leave California and Oregon open to slavery. In April 1847, opposing an effort by John C. Calhoun to leave the latter open to the peculiar institution, Polk suspected the South Carolinian of pandering to southern slaveholders to advance presidential aspirations: "He is wholly selfish, & I am satisfied has no patriotism." From Polk's viewpoint, pro- and antislavery partisans alike were exploiting the issue of slavery for political gain: "Both desire to mount slavery as a hobby, and hope to secure the election of their favourite upon it."[16]

Those attitudes notwithstanding, Polk, in his quest for new lands, was also sufficiently aware of political exigencies to, by his lights, balance acquisitions of slave and free territories. And husbanding political capital, he commenced his expansionist initiatives successively, not simultaneously. Far from being unbridled in time and space, each annexation project he undertook was discrete, limited in scope, and bound by considerations of practical politics.[17] As a consequence, readers coming to Polk's writings in search of musings à la Thomas Jefferson on philosophy, the arts, and literature, expressed with the literary flourishes of an eighteenth-century *philosophe,* will come away disappointed. But those who seek the words, however plain spoken, of a Machiavellian political maestro will find, in his private words, precisely those.

James Knox Polk (1795–1849) in an 1846 portrait by George Healy. From 1845 to 1849, Polk served as the eleventh U.S. president. A lawyer and former Tennessee congressman and governor, Polk as president, through war and diplomacy, increased by one-third the area of the United States, giving it a coast-to-coast breadth, thus rendering it a continental nation-state. Though historians often associate his name with the phrase "Manifest Destiny," no record has been located of his ever using the term. (Polk Ancestral Home)

James Knox Polk and his wife, Sarah Childress Polk (1803–1891), in a joint portrait likely taken in 1849 by daguerreotypist Mathew Brady. (Polk Ancestral Home)

An 1844 campaign banner touts that year's Democratic party's ticket of James Polk (left) and vice presidential running mate, former Philadelphia mayor and U.S. senator George Dallas (right). At the Democratic convention, the candidacy of Martin Van Buren, former president and nomination front-runner, faded when opponents implemented a rule that required a two-thirds majority to select a candidate, and the convention deadlocked. Not until its ninth ballot was the nominee, James K. Polk, chosen—an unexpected event, widely believed to have occasioned the first usage in presidential politics of the term "dark horse." The above banner includes one of the sobriquets by which Polk was by then known, "The Young Hickory"—a moniker that alluded to Polk's mentor Andrew Jackson, "Old Hickory." The banner was created by lithographer Nathaniel Currier whose firm, after 1850 when he was joined by a partner, James Ives, became Currier and Ives. (Library of Congress)

HENRY CLAY.
Eleventh President of the United States

Henry Clay (1777–1852) of Kentucky, the Whig party's 1844 presidential nominee, promised that if he won the presidency, he would serve only one term. Democratic candidate Polk duplicated Clay's pledge. In the November election, Polk defeated Clay by less than two percent in the popular vote, but by a 170 to 105 margin in the Electoral College. Above the optimistic phrase "Eleventh President of the United States" in this campaign lithograph—but illegible in this reproduction—are the words "nominated for." (Library of Congress)

John Tyler (1790–1862), Polk's immediate predecessor as president, in a circa 1860-65 portrait of unknown origin. The Virginian became the tenth U.S. president upon the death of Whig Benjamin Harrison, for whom Tyler had served as vice-president. Though nominally a Whig when he became president, he was soon expelled from that party. It was Tyler who lit the fuse that ignited the U.S. war with Mexico over which Polk would preside. On February 28, 1845, four days before Polk took office, Congress, at Tyler's behest, passed a joint resolution extending the Republic of Texas a long-sought invitation to apply for U.S. annexation. Mexico's government, having never recognized Texas's claimed independence, considered the invitation a belligerent act. (Library of Congress)

Two political cartoons by H. Bucholzer (left and next page) reflect the vagaries of Polk's road to the presidency. "Footrace, Pennsylvania Avenue" captures the conventional wisdom early in the summer of 1844 that Whig nominee Henry Clay would win the election. "Stakes $25,000" refers to the presidential salary. Whig nominee Clay leads the race, with Polk lagging behind and stumbling in a pothole. Incumbent president John Tyler lags behind Polk. Tyler subsequently withdrew, in August, from the race. In the foreground offering comments are vice presidential candidate Theodore Frelinghuysen, and Whig senator Daniel Webster.

FOOTRACE, PENSYLVANIA AVENUE.
Stakes $25,000.

"Texas Coming In," 1844, reflects how the presidential race had changed by the following fall after concerns about Texas had come to dominate the contest, with Polk favoring its annexation and Clay appearing to vacillate on the issue. "Salt River," depicted in the cartoon, was a common metaphor of the era, for failure or embarrassment. Polk, standing ashore, celebrates as Texas patriots (left to right) Stephen Austin and Sam Houston ride a wheeled steamboat-like vehicle across the bridge. Their vehicle is being drawn to the opposite bank by a rope pulled by Clay and other Whigs who otherwise appear helpless in Salt River. (Library of Congress)

Though the likeness of its main subject is unrecognizable—which figure on the platform is the new president?—this engraving from the *Illustrated News of London* purports to depict Polk, on March 4, 1845, amid a stormy downpour, taking the presidential oath, on a platform beside the U.S. capitol's East Portico. U.S. Supreme Court chief justice Roger B. Taney administered the oath. At forty-nine, Polk was then the youngest man to ever attain the presidency, and ten years younger than the average age of earlier presidents. Polk's inaugural address—delivered by that day's custom, *before* the oath of office—reaffirmed campaign promises to aggressively advance U.S. interests in Oregon and Texas. To the platform's left looms a statue, "The Discovery of America," by sculptor Luigi Persico, installed in 1844 and removed in 1958. (Library of Congress)

Two cartoons (here and next page)—both by Philadelphia artist Edward Williams Clay (1792–1857)—reflect early and widespread public speculation over the directions that Polk's presidency would take. "The patriots getting their beans," which appeared in 1845, shortly after Polk's election, presents his various Democratic allies and potential beneficiaries of White House patronage promoting their respective causes and personal aspiration as the president-elect sits with hands folded, serenely oblivious to the commotion. (Library of Congress)

THE PATRIOTS GETTING THEIR BEANS.

Edward Williams Clay's "Polk's Dream," published in 1846, early in the Tennessean's presidency, captures the public's still unsettled view of the new chief of state's intentions: as the president sleeps, assorted figures—ranging from former president Andrew Jackson to the Devil—visit in a dream, each pressing upon Polk his own political wish. (Library of Congress)

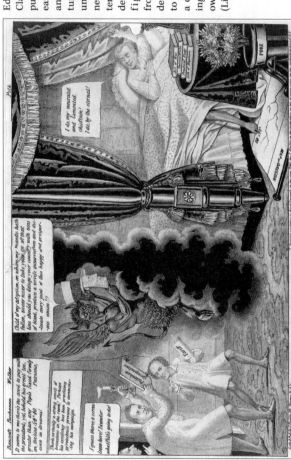

POLK'S DREAM.

James K. Polk and cabinet in a daguerreotype taken by John Plumbe, Jr. in 1846. The image constitutes the earliest known interior photograph of the White House, as well as the first of a President with his cabinet. Standing, left to right: Cave Johnson, George Bancroft; seated, left to right: John Y. Mason, William L. Marcy, President Polk, Robert J. Walker. James Buchanan, secretary of state, is missing. As with all daguerreotypes, this is a mirror image. (Polk Ancestral Home)

War News from Mexico, an 1848 painting by Richard Canton Woodville, captures the public excitement that, in many quarters, greeted U.S. victories in the Mexican War. Note, however, on right, the black man and the little girl—presumably his daughter—both less well dressed than the jubilant men on the porch, and who sit impassively. The victories did not bode well for African Americans—or the Union. (Crystal Bridges Museum of American Art)

Journalist and Democratic party activist John L. O'Sullivan (1813–1895), in an engraving published in *Harper's Weekly* in 1874. Conventional wisdom associates Polk's presidency, indeed his very name, with "Manifest Destiny." But the locution was coined in 1845 by O'Sullivan. Writing in the *United States Magazine and Democratic Review*, a literary and political journal that he co-owned and edited, O'Sullivan, while calling for U.S. annexation of Texas, argued that it is "our manifest destiny to overspread the continent allotted by Providence for the free development of our yearly multiplying millions." Soon popularized by the era's penny press, Manifest Destiny never received a precise definition. A Procrustean phrase, more often invoked in its day by those selling newspapers than by policymakers, it came to refer to an unbridled, in most cases east-to-west, U.S. expansionism ordained by a Protestant, Anglo-Saxon God. That most of the lands eyed for conquest were home to native peoples and other non–Anglo-Saxon populations mattered little to Manifest Destiny's adherents. Nor, for that matter, did U.S. settlers always proceed from east to west. Often, as with those Texas-bound pioneers, many moved from northeast to southwest; in California, with many arrivals coming via the Pacific, newcomers often moved from west to east. (*Harper's Weekly*)

Thomas Hart Benton (1782–1858) in a daguerreotype created by Mathew Brady between 1845 and 1850. Benton served as U.S. senator from Missouri from 1821 to 1851. During his Senate years, he became a principal architect of federal policy in the West. Due to his in-depth knowledge of the region, his prowess in creating policies there often eclipsed contemporary presidents, including Polk. (Library of Congress)

Explorer John Charles Frémont (1813–1890) in a circa mid-nineteenth engraving by T. Knight after a daguerreotype by Mathew Brady. During the 1840s, Frémont led a series of federally sponsored exploring expeditions into the American West. His published journals proved wildly popular, reshaped popular conceptions of the region and sparked the first mass emigration by U.S. citizens there. Unlike Thomas Jefferson, who, as president, planned explorers Lewis and Clark famous Corps of Discovery expedition (1804–6) into the Far West, Polk played no active role in planning the Frémont expedition conducted during his presidency. The Georgia-born explorer was a son-in-law of Senator Benton, who did play a large role in his career and the shaping of his expeditions. (Library of Congress)

This cartoon—published in December 1848 or early 1849, and possibly drawn by S. Lee Perkins—tapped into fears of the gold recently discovered in the new U.S. possession of California. U.S. president Zachary Taylor is depicted as an eagle; and Polk as a snake. Each warns against approaching foreign interlopers—including Queen Victoria of the United Kingdom, French president Louise-Philippe, Spain's Queen Isabella II, and Russian Czar Nicholas I. (Library of Congress)

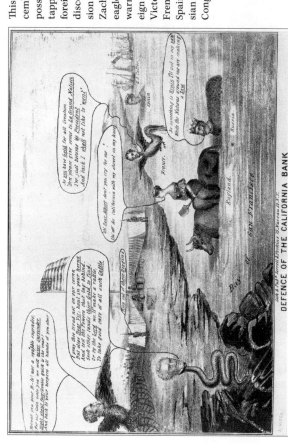

FOR PRESIDENT OF THE PEOPLE

ZACHARY TAYLOR

About party creeds let party zealots fight
He cant be wrong whose life is in the right . —

An 1850 lithograph by J.L. Rogers depicts that year's Whig candidate for president, Zachary Taylor (1784–1850), who succeeded Polk to become the twelfth U.S. president. Taylor had served as the first of Polk's two successive chief generals in the Mexican War. This lithograph—reflecting Taylor's indeterminate party affiliation when he began his presidential campaign—includes the couplet: "About party creeds let party zealots fight / He cant be wrong whose life is in the right." (Library of Congress)

In an 1849 portrait of James Polk by photographer Mathew Brady, the ravages taken on the president by declining health and the duties of office are plainly evident. Months earlier, in a letter to a friend, Polk reflected that, the "country is prosperous in a degree almost without an example, and if the war can be brought to a successful termination, a long course of prosperity is before us, and I shall retire at the close of my term, with the satisfaction of believing I have rendered my country some service." But the future failed to redeem those expectations. Polk's retirement was cruelly brief. Marking the briefest post-presidency retirement in U. S. history, he died in June 1849, three months after leaving the White House. And the legacy of peace and prosperity that he envisioned for the country, which his policies had so enlarged, was also short lived. Within a dozen years of his leaving the White House, a conflict erupted that violently divided the United States. (James K. Polk Ancestral Home)

THE AUTOCRAT

Ironies abound. Historians associate Polk with bestowing upon the United States its modern coast-to-coast breadth, and today his name resonates in myriad place names west of the Mississippi. But those associations notwithstanding, this president who dispatched explorer John C. Frémont's Third Expedition into the Far West, and who subsequently brought that realm under U.S. dominion, had scant intellectual curiosity about the region.

He never personally ventured into the trans-Missouri frontier or to the Pacific Coast. Indeed, Frémont's father-in-law, Senator Thomas Hart Benton, not Polk, was, as he had been for earlier presidents, the intellectual architect of the Polk administration's Far West policies. Moreover, it was Frémont's explorations that revealed the West to be more topographically and ecologically variegated than earlier believed and exploded the long-held misconception that a wasteland—the "Great American Desert"—covered most of the region. And Polk never had with Frémont the sort of close relationship and shared intense interests in the West—its geography, ethnography, and flora and fauna—that Thomas Jefferson had with Meriwether Lewis, one of the several explorers that Jefferson as president dispatched into Western climes. Indeed, unlike Jefferson, who personally prepared instructions for Lewis and Clark's 1804–6 Corps of Discovery into the Far West, Polk had little if any direct involvement in planning the exploration that Frémont conducted during his presidency.

Beyond that, while the government-sponsored explorations of the 1840s that secured Frémont's reputation are often associated with Polk's administration, the successive western surveys of that era in which he participated—surveys that cohered into a sustained program of geographical investigation—were initially led by French-born explorer Joseph Nicollet. Moreover, those expeditions actually began in the late 1830s under the presidency of Martin Van Buren (later, a Polk rival); continued under the Whig presidents William Henry Harrison and John Tyler; and concluded under Democrat Polk. Afterwards, of less historical significance, Frémont, in 1848–49 and 1853–54, led two disastrous federally sponsored expeditions in the San Juan mountains of southern Colorado and northern New Mexico, in vain searches for a central route across the Rockies, a route favored by Senator Benton, for a proposed St. Louis-to-San Francisco transcontinental rail-line.[1]

Polk, for his part, seldom strayed far from Tennessee or Washington, D.C. During his entire lifetime, he never traveled abroad. A summer 1847 tour of New England conducted during his presidency represented his single foray into that region. On the eve of that outing, he wrote to an associate, "After my constant confinement here for more than two years, with the exception of less than a week, last summer, I feel that some little respite from my public labours and cares, will be proper, if not necessary."[2]

The avoidance of travel went beyond affections for home and hearth. Polk was devoted to the work of governance. Despite frequent health woes, he possessed a work ethic of the same magnitude as that of, say, Benjamin Franklin or Thomas Edison. Indeed, for defensible reasons, he saw himself as indispensable to the competent running of state affairs. One may contest Polk's policies and the results they produced, but his intelligence, discretion, and political acumen—lapses notwithstanding—are indisputable. At his shrewdest, he conducted himself as the formidable chess master who, in his head, plays multiple moves ahead of his opponents.

Similar to British prime minister Robert Peel, among his contemporary counterparts on the Atlantic's far side,[3] Polk often circumvented cabinet officers. When something he deemed truly important required tending, he often saw himself as the best man for the job and otherwise supervised subordinates closely. To his diary, the president confided, "I prefer to supervise the whole operations of the Government myself rather than entrust the public business to subordinates, and this makes my duties very great."[4] A tireless worker, Polk had few if any hobbies or outside interests. Indeed, as Michael Cohen, my colleague on the Polk correspondence project, recently remarked, his sole recreation seems to have been, fortuitously for historians, keeping up with correspondence.

Just as Polk's successes eventually quelled debates about his methods, so his association—however ill founded—with the hyperbole of Manifest Destiny, along with his triumphs in expanding America's territorial bounty, have obscured ironies and outright disappointments that attended his turn in office. Those disappointments included his failure to purchase Cuba. They also included his administration's failure, despite vigorous efforts, to win statehood for California and to establish a territorial government for New Mexico. Cuba would never enter the federal Union. But those other aforementioned tasks would be left for successor presidents and not resolved until the Compromise of 1850—itself a fragile piece of political handiwork that in the end provided only a brief surcease to tensions resulting from Polk's Mexican Cession of 1848. Indeed, simmering debates over the future of slavery in the United States—debates brought to a boil by the Mexican Cession—eventually produced perhaps the central irony of Polk's legacy: A president ostensibly devoted to U.S. nationalism ultimately sectionalized the nation's politics, creating a geographical fracturing that soon led to civil war.

It's also noteworthy that Polk presided over an era of intense technological innovation in the United States. Emblematic of that progress, his nomination in 1844 was the first major news story reported by telegraph. He was also the first sitting president to be photographed in the White House. And his presidency made its share of improvements to the nation's domestic life. Notably, Postmaster General Cave Johnson introduced America's first postage stamp. Until then, recipients of mail had borne the burden of paying postage due; postage stamps thus simplified and streamlined communications.[5]

Polk's first navy secretary, George Bancroft, established the United States Naval Academy in Annapolis, Maryland, an act of far-reaching consequences in modernizing and expanding the global reach of the nation's maritime force. Likewise, Polk's establishment of the Independent Treasury (his preferred term was "constitutional treasury") served to modernize—or perhaps, more accurately, lay the groundwork for the later modernization of—the nation's finances. The Independent Treasury Act of 1846 mandated that henceforth all federal funds were to be kept, not in private state banks or national corporations, but in vaults owned by the federal government. Consistent with Polk's Jacksonian convictions, all transactions were to be conducted in hard money. The Independent Treasury remained in operation until 1913, when it was replaced with the Federal Reserve System.

In most matters, however, Polk opposed his longtime Whig opponent Henry Clay's "American System," a program that favored protectionist tariffs, centralized control of banking and currency, and federal support for industry and infrastructure—"internal improvements." In opposing such measures, Polk, to the end of his days, displayed unshakable fealty to his mentor Andrew Jackson.

THE HISTORIAN AND
THE PRESIDENT

Oft-told stories die hard. Newly published letters to and from Polk—and close examination of what has become a defining anecdote of his presidency—lift the veil on a more complex story than usually assumed: a president and administration with policies driven by a broad range of concerns, producing results often overlooked by historians. Even triumphs, as it turns out, often led to unintended consequences and problems.

Why such scant attention to the lost debates, challenges, and unintended consequences of Polk's turn as president? During much of the twentieth century and continuing into the twenty-first, a widely quoted anecdote bolstered the Tennessean's reputation as a politician of set goals—and a master of outcomes. The anecdote portrays Polk, around the time of his inauguration, as having "raised his hand high in the air." Then, "bringing it down with force on his thigh," he enumerated what he predicted would be the "four great measures" of his administration: the acquisition of some or all of the Oregon Country, the acquisition of California, a reduction in tariffs (to stimulate free trade), and the permanent establishment of the aforementioned Independent Treasury. In four years, Polk accomplished all four objectives.

The anecdote comes from Massachusetts-born teacher, politician, and historian George Bancroft (1800–1891). A graduate of Harvard College who pursued postgraduate studies in Germany, Bancroft devoted most of his professional career to writing books chronicling U.S. colonial history. His books sold well and made him successful and wealthy. Intermittently, he also pursued careers in politics and diplomacy. Beyond his years with Polk, Bancroft, during the 1860s, became a Republican and, following the Civil War, served as minister to Prussia, 1867–71, and to the German Empire, 1871–74.

Bancroft was five years younger than Polk. In many ways, the sociable and worldly historian from New England and the retiring and sometimes provincial Tennessean were a study in contrasts. Indeed, emblematic of the lofty circles that he inhabited for most of his life, Bancroft, following his student years in Europe, conducted a grand tour in which he called on luminaries such as Lord Byron, Georg Wilhelm Friedrich Hegel, and Johann Wolfgang von Goethe.

Traits Bancroft and Polk shared, however, drew them together. Both, after all, were well educated; moreover, both were committed to the Democratic party—and each, in his own way, was possessed of a robust Anglophobia. Bancroft's appointment in 1837 by President Martin Van Buren as collector of customs for the port of Boston had marked his arrival in Democratic party politics. In 1844, he was that party's nominee for Massachusetts governor, but lost in the general election. That same year, Bancroft helped Polk secure the Democratic nomination for president. And, soon enough, the New Englander began his service to the new president—as navy secretary in March 1845 and as minister to the United Kingdom after September 1846.

Moreover, during Bancroft's tenure with the Polk administration, he increasingly professed to view the nation's territorial expansion as offering remedies for its problems—social, moral, political. Up until then, according to Bancroft's biographer Lilian Handlin, the New Englander had promoted advancements for the rights of labor as the central remedy for the nation's woes. After, however, joining the Polk administration, Handlin writes, he increasingly embraced a new curative for those problems. "Having argued once that the elevation of the working classes would cure all social maladjustments (never bothering to say how), Bancroft in 1845 made territorial growth the panacea for most of the nation's problems."

Trafficking in an agrarianism resonant among American thinkers—before, during, and after Bancroft's day, from Jefferson to Frederick Jackson Turner—he came to view the annexation of new lands as essential to the nation's future. As Handlin summarized Bancroft's view of the regenerative benefits of such policies,

> More land would alleviate hardships caused by an expanding economy. Productive outlets for commercial growth would drain off excess riches and diminish the dangers of envy, greed and political unrest. An end to the influence of rapacious manufacturers, to low wages, to periodic recessions, and to the

overextension of capital would be among the other by-products, also vindicating the immutable laws of a free economy.

Bancroft's thigh-slapping anecdote made an early—perhaps its earliest—appearance in a typescript titled "Biographical sketch of James K. Polk" (c. late 1880s), now among Bancroft's papers at the New York Public Library. In an addendum to an article on Polk published in *Appletons' Cyclopædia of American Biography* (1888), Bancroft, though he does not repeat the anecdote, nonetheless praises his former boss: "His administration, viewed from the standpoint of results, was perhaps the greatest in our national history, certainly one of the greatest."[1]

In 1889, Bancroft's thigh-slapping story—seemingly presenting the most ambitious to-do list in U.S. history—was repeated, with slight variations, in historian James Schouler's *History of the United States of America, under the Constitution.* As he indicates in a footnote, Schouler learned the story from a February 1887 letter from Bancroft. After repeating the anecdote, Schouler, borrowing almost verbatim a passage from that Bancroft letter, concludes, "And history should record that Polk entered on his official duties with the immovable purpose of carrying every one of these measures into effect, and before his term had ended accomplished them all."[2]

Further ratifying the anecdote, Eugene Irving McCormac—citing Schouler as his source—recounted it in his 1922 book *James K. Polk: A Political Biography,* the first full-fledged modern study of the Polk presidency.

McCormac thus stamped upon Bancroft's foggy recollection what seemed to be an imprimatur of solid provenance—and thusly concluded his study: "No other president took his task more seriously nor spent his energies more freely for his country; and few, indeed, have done more to increase the power and prestige of the nation."[3]

Echoing Bancroft, Schouler, and McCormac, many, though not all, subsequent U.S. historians have accorded Polk's presidency similarly favorable assessments. Most of those assayers have repeated the anecdote or, minimally, assumed its core premise—that Polk devoted his presidency to achieving the anecdote's four goals. In 1948, Arthur M. Schlesinger Sr. asked other historians to rank all U.S. presidents by their performance as chief executive. When their responses were averaged, Polk finished in tenth place. "Polk set himself certain precise objectives to be achieved while he was President, and achieve them he did," wrote Schlesinger approvingly. When Schlesinger repeated the exercise in 1962, Polk fared even better, finishing eighth. When his son, Arthur M. Schlesinger Jr., repeated the survey in 1997, Polk finished at number nine.[4]

The anecdote and its resultant assessment resonated—and continues to resonate—widely. "A great President," Harry S. Truman, a former president himself, remarked of Polk. "Said what he intended to do and did it."[5] Similarly, Republican strategist Karl Rove, assessing during the summer of 2012 the prospects for Mitt Romney, his party's presidential nominee of that year, found parallels between Polk's presidency and what Rove viewed as the likely success of a Romney administration. "He [Romney] will be like Polk," Rove said, adding that Polk "is one of the near greats, and we don't recognize [him]." Even so, Rove added, "we've begun to recognize him in recent years. But here's a guy who ran, and he said he was going to do four things."[6] Indeed, Polk's alleged four goals pronouncement—with and without the thigh slap—has become so ubiquitous that it has found its way into U.S. history textbooks and, in at least one case, into the lyrics of a popular song.[7]

But the continual recounting of the anecdote and Polk's consequent high ratings come in spite of many historians' belief that his expansionist policies led irrevocably to the American Civil War, the conflict that ensued a dozen years after he departed Washington. Furthermore, as noted herein, Polk's correspondence yields a more complex account of his administration than does Bancroft's anecdote.

What's going on here? For starters, as it turns out, Bancroft's presidential thigh-slapping anecdote hangs by the thinnest of evidentiary threads. So far as is known, Bancroft did not write of Polk's enumeration-of-goals pronouncement until the late 1880s—four decades after Polk's presidency.

As the nineteenth century waned, so too did Polk's reputation. Many historians, as noted above, had by then come to view the Mexican War as having led to the American Civil War. Mostly, however, Polk's presidency settled into obscurity. Polk had hoped that his war secretary, William L. Marcy, would write a history of the administration, but Marcy ultimately declined.[8] Moreover, historians who did recount the Mexican War and other events of the era tended to rely mainly on Whig sources; and to the degree that Polk was mentioned at all in such accounts, he was portrayed as a surrogate for others.

Indeed, in 1886, the young historian and future president Theodore Roosevelt dismissed Polk's presidency on just those grounds. In a biography of Thomas Hart Benton that he published that year, Roosevelt presented Polk's Oregon treaty as issuing from a capitulation to repeated demands by partisans and, simultaneously, Secretary of State James Buchanan's fear of upsetting the British. As for Texas and the Mexican War, Roosevelt wrote, Polk's actions in those realms resulted from his being bullied by expansionists—being barely an actor in the drama—into actions that produced problems left for subsequent presidents to solve. In short, inveighed Roosevelt, the "administration was neither capable nor warlike, however well disposed to bluster."[9] Complaining of such depictions, McCormac, in his 1922 study of Polk, lamented that such portrayals presented the chief executive as the "mere tool of more capable intriguers." In the end, the historian complained, "the President was not even given the credit usually accorded to a successful conspirator."[10]

Historian Frederick Jackson Turner's landmark paper "The Significance of the Frontier in American History," delivered in 1893, bore further witness to the eclipse of Polk's reputation. Turner accorded white settlers the leading role in securing the West for the United States. But tellingly, the list of political leaders whose views on national expansion Turner deemed worthy of mention—among others, Washington, Jefferson, Jackson, Calhoun, William Henry Harrison, and Benton—did not include Polk. Indeed, adding insult to injury, Turner singled out Polk's contemporary Benton as "the man of widest views of the destiny of the West."[11]

By the late nineteenth century, such neglect—and condemnations—of Polk were common. And George Bancroft, as the only surviving member of Polk's cabinet, felt a personal sting in both. According to Bancroft biographer Lilian Handlin, the historian genuinely believed that policies enacted by his former boss had richly benefitted the nation and even led to the Union's victory in the American Civil War. Thus, during the 1880s, Bancroft resolved to write a long-contemplated biography of Polk, a work intended to vindicate its subject against his neglect by historians and a rising chorus of critics.

Of that resolve to burnish Polk's reputation, we can only speculate about the role played in its making by Bancroft's pondering of Otto von Bismarck and public veneration of the Prussian statesman. In the late 1860s and early seventies, during his diplomatic posting in Berlin, Bancroft and Bismarck had become close friends. Unlike Polk, however, Bismarck had won enduring admiration, in many quarters, for the wars and diplomacy over which he had presided—policies of national aggrandizement that had united a nation and created an empire. Indeed, during his time in Berlin, the Junker's illiberal tendencies notwithstanding, Bancroft had become enamored of Bismarck and his achievements, even likening him to George Washington, for his role in forging the unification of Germany. Against that background, it requires scant effort to imagine that, as Bancroft pondered public veneration of Bismarck—and contrasted it with the eleventh president's disrepute in the United States—it must, at some point, have occurred to him that, with the right historian to tell Polk's story, Bancroft's countrymen might yet venerate—venerate as Germans did their Iron Chancellor—the plain-spoken Tennessean who, during his four-year term, created a coast-to-coast nation-state.

By all rights, Bancroft, a professional historian, might have seemed the obvious person to write the history of the Polk administration. Polk, however, did not hold that view. In May 1849, after leaving the White House and weeks before his death, Polk wrote to William Marcy and beseeched his former war secretary to take up the task, arguing that his knowledge "of the facts and the considerations, upon which we acted"—particularly after Bancroft left for London—"would be more extensive and minute" than that of Bancroft. The historian, after all, in the fall of 1846, had left his post in Washington as navy secretary to take up a diplomatic posting in London.

Marcy admired Polk but ultimately declined the entreaty, believing that praise from a member of the Tennessean's cabinet would be discounted by the reading public. In the years after Marcy declined the offer and the former president's death, Sarah Polk approached several others about the project—including Henry Stephens Randall, author of an early biography of Thomas Jefferson; Ransom Hooker Gillet, a former congressman and Polk associate; and John Cadwalader, a well-regarded Philadelphia jurist and politician. All expressed interest but for various reasons none of the three embarked upon the biography.

And so, in 1887, upon learning that George Bancroft was interested in writing a Polk biography, Sarah welcomed the news. That spring, Bancroft visited Nashville. There, under Sarah's auspices, he examined various papers

of the late president. Afterwards, Sarah—assisted by journalist and Polk associate Jeremiah George Harris, author
of an 1844 campaign biography of Polk—packed up the
documents that Bancroft had examined, as well as other
presidential materials, and shipped them to Bancroft's residence in Washington to allow him to copy them. By that
August, Bancroft had returned the papers to the former
first lady.[12]

During the coming months, in Washington and at another residence in Newport, Rhode Island, Bancroft pored
over the materials. In the end, however, failing energy
and memory prevented his completion of the Polk biography and other projects begun during those years, including a biography of Shakespeare and an essay on Milton.
Bancroft's resolve to write a Polk apologia produced scant
results—mainly the article published in *Appletons' Cyclopædia* and the never-published typescript in which Bancroft
presented the thigh-slapping anecdote.[13]

In that typescript's recounting of the alleged incident,
Bancroft balks at asserting that he himself heard Polk
make the pronouncement; he states only that it was made
in the presence of "one of those whom he had selected for
one of the departments of the government." In his February
1887 letter to Schouler, however, Bancroft presents himself
as the original source of the anecdote—indeed as one of
only two witnesses to the alleged exchange ("In a private
conversation of President Polk with me . . ."). Bancroft's ca-
geyness about the source of the anecdote, forty years after
the fact, seems odd. If he were witness to the pronouncement, why the hesitancy to declare that fact? Any pledge of
confidentiality given by Bancroft to Polk, after all, would
have been breached by Bancroft's own disclosure of the

story. Besides, why would Polk require—and Bancroft feel bound to maintain—any pledge of confidentiality on a story so flattering to Polk?

Chronological inconsistencies also dog Bancroft's account of the conversation. In the first of its two recountings in his unpublished Polk typescript, Bancroft dates the conversation as having occurred "after" Polk's inauguration; in its second recounting in that same document, Bancroft places the moment "just before the inauguration." In the letter to Schouler, Bancroft sets the conversation "soon after he had taken the oath of office." The chronology is not made less muddy by the fact that Bancroft—writing, from Washington, to his wife on February 17, 1845, four weeks before Polk's inauguration—was still waiting to learn what post he would occupy in the new administration; to her, he complained, "The president elect keeps his own counsels most closely"—hardly an observation suggesting that the Tennessean was, at least in Bancroft's presence, a font of audacious boasts; or that Bancroft was a confidant of the incoming chief.

Of course, historians rarely have unimpeachable sources, and witnesses to historical events cannot be expected to be able to withstand the sort of rigorous cross-examination to which a skilled lawyer, during a trial, subjects a witness for the opposing side. Nonetheless, even if one accepts the notion that the elderly Bancroft was making a good-faith effort to recall, as best he could, a long-ago incident, such inconsistencies hardly inspire confidence in the octogenarian's powers of recollection.

Beyond those circumstances, no recounting of or allusion to the incident—or any similar summation of policy goals—appears in Polk's diary. Admittedly, Polk's diary begins in late August 1845, five months after he took office. Then again, no references to such presidential foresight appear in his correspondence thus far surveyed by the current editors of the *Correspondence of James K. Polk*. Nor have we located accounts of or allusions to the pronouncement in any other Polk-related contemporary documents.[14]

Also curious is the anecdote's omission of Texas. Although nominally addressed by Polk's predecessor, John Tyler, the matter of Texas, when Polk took office, ranked among the new president's most pressing challenges in both domestic and foreign policy. In February 1845, North Carolina U.S. senator Willie P. Mangum wrote to an associate, "The arrival of the President elect has given a powerful impulse to party action on this subject.— He is for Texas, Texas, Texas; & talks of but little else." Indeed, at that juncture, sharpening concerns, many in Washington focused on possible British and French intrigues in Texas as well as fears of a Mexican invasion of the republic.[15]

Polk eventually clarified Texas' status as a new state in the Union. But the means he took to resolve the matter and its consequences, a war and a new slave state, both exacerbating North-South sectional tensions, sparked controversy. Loud public debates raged during Polk's day. More quietly, among historians, they continued well into the 1880s, when Bancroft presented the thigh-slapping anecdote. But in Bancroft's anecdote, Polk makes no mention of Texas or the Mexican War. Instead, in its sole nod to the war, the list of presidential goals includes a less controversial consequence of that conflict, the United States' acquisition of California, which eventually entered the Union as a free state in 1850.

Curiously—and contradicting the objectives set forth in Bancroft's anecdote—Polk himself, in October 1845, disavowed any resolve to acquire California. In a diary entry, he records a conversation in which he revealed that unless a third-party country—the United Kingdom—sought to acquire the Mexican province, he would be content for it to remain under title to its present owner, the Republic of Mexico. Equally remarkable, the conversation, with Senator Thomas Hart Benton, took place on October 24—presumably months after the "four great measures" recitation described by Bancroft as having taken place early in or even before Polk's presidency:

> The conversation then turned on California, on which I remarked that Great Brittain [sic] had her eye on that country and intended to possess it if she could, but that the people of the U.S. would not willingly permit California to pass into the possession of any new colony planted by Great Brittain or any foreign monarchy, and that in asserting Mr. Monroe's doctrine, I had California & the fine bay of San Francisco as much in view as Oregon. Col. Benton agreed that no Foreign Power ought to be permitted to colonize California, any more than they would be to colonize Cuba. As long as Cuba remained in the possession of the present Government we would not object, but if a powerful foreign power was about to possess it, we would not permit it. On the same footing we would place California.

Clearly, Polk's priority regarding California during his October 24, 1845, meeting with Benton, emphasized maintenance of the diplomatic status quo—"Mr. Monroe's doctrine"—not U.S. attainment of the Mexican province.

Of course, Polk eventually did bring California into the federal Union. And to be fair, perhaps along the way his resolve to acquire that distant Pacific realm ebbed and flowed. Perhaps he began his presidency determined to acquire California; by October 1845, the resolve had lessened, and by 1848, it had been rekindled. Even so, the construction of Bancroft's "four great measures" anecdote—with its omission of Texas and Mexico but its resolute inclusion of California—gives the ostensibly spontaneous moment of presidential bravado a studied ex post facto feel.

However, yet another document—a recently surfaced letter from an admirer to President Polk— does more fully comport with the contents of Bancroft's recollection of Polk's enunciation of the "measures" by which his administration would be remembered. More than that, the letter— re-configuring the same goals enunciated in that famous anecdote, and adding, for good measure, another—the administration's ostensible adherence to "strict" Constitutional principles—actually inventories not four but six "measures." The admirer thus writes,

> The establishment of the constitutional Treasury, the overthrow of protection, the adjustment of our boundary, the rigidly strict construction of the Constitution, the annexation of Texas, the purchase of New Mexico & California form a series of measures, the like of which can hardly ever again be crowded into one administration of four years, & which in the eyes of posterity will single yours out among the administrations of the century.

The presidential admirer penned his letter on August 5, 1848—eight months before the Polk's administration's conclusion. His missive included no allusion to the president having earlier spoken of the achievements as goals. Nevertheless, its contents and diction strongly resemble those attributed, four decades later, to Polk himself in Bancroft's "four measures" anecdote.

The author of that admiring letter from August 1848? George Bancroft.[16]

Sarah Childress Polk (1803–1891) appears in this lithograph, published in 1846, by Nathaniel Currier. The refined daughter of a prosperous Tennessee planter and businessman, she married James Polk in 1824. Possessed of an advanced education and formidable intelligence, Sarah counseled her husband in matters of both business and politics. The couple had no children, but the portrait of their White House life that emerges from letters includes a retinue of nieces and nephews from Tennessee staying for extended visits. In the years after former war secretary William Marcy declined to write a history of her husband's presidency, Sarah Polk approached several others about the project. In 1887, upon learning of George Bancroft's interest in writing a Polk biography, Sarah welcomed the news. (James K. Polk Ancestral Home)

Emanuel Leutze's allegorical mural *Westward the Course of Empire Takes its Way* (1862) hangs in the U.S. Capitol. Reflecting the diminishment and otherwise neglect of Polk's reputation during that era, Leutze's painting does not depict the eleventh president. (Library of Congress)

A circa 1873 chromo-lithograph by George Crofutt after John Gast's allegorical *American Progress* (1872). Like Leutze's earlier *Westward the Course of Empire Takes its Way*, Gast's paean to U.S. expansion into the West does not reference Polk. (Crystal Springs Museum)

Historian Frederick Jackson Turner (1861–1932) in a circa 1917 photograph of unknown origin. Turner's landmark paper, "The Significance of the Frontier in American History," delivered in 1893, had a profound influence on generations of historians of the United States. It also bore further witness to the eclipse of Polk's reputation. Turner accorded white settlers the leading role in securing the West for the United States. But tellingly, the list of political leaders whose views on national expansion Turner deemed worthy of mention did not include Polk. (Library of Congress)

Polk's war secretary William Marcy (1786–1857) in a circa 1840 to 1857 portrait of unknown origin. The former New York governor and U.S. senator numbered among Polk's inner circle, and he was Polk's first choice to write a history of the administration. George Bancroft, a professional historian, might have seemed the logical person for the project. But after Bancroft left his navy secretary post in 1846 to move to London to become U.S. minister to the United Kingdom, he became removed from the administration's day-to-day activities. In May 1849—months after leaving office and weeks before his death—Polk urged Marcy to undertake the book, flattering him that it "would be more extensive and minute" than any study Bancroft could produce. The New Yorker, however, declined, writing the former president that praise of the administration from a member of its cabinet would be discounted by the reading public. (Library of Congress)

Massachusetts native George Bancroft (1800–1891), in an 1846 daguerreotype by John Plumbe, Jr. The historian, teacher and diplomat served President Polk, successively, as Navy secretary and U.S. minister to the United Kingdom. Later, after becoming a Republican, Bancroft served as minister to Prussia (1867–71) and to the German Empire (1871–74). The above daguerreotype captured Bancroft after he joined the Polk administration. (National Portrait Gallery, Smithsonian Institution)

Otto von Bismarck (1815–1898), in a circa 1870 engraving after a painting by Alonzo Chappel. During George Bancroft's diplomatic posting in Berlin after the Civil War, he came to know and admire the revered Prussian statesman. Shortly thereafter, Bancroft resolved to write a long-contemplated biography of Polk, a work intended to vindicate its subject against neglect by historians and a rising chorus of critics. Might Bancroft's resolve have arisen from his pondering of Bismarck's ongoing veneration? Might Bancroft have thought that, with the right historian to tell Polk's story, his countrymen might yet venerate the eleventh president much as many Germans did their Iron Chancellor, who had used wars and diplomacy to create an empire? (Library of Congress)

A photograph, by Frances Benjamin Johnston, shows Bancroft during the 1880s, when, as an octogenarian and the only surviving member of Polk's cabinet, he sought to burnish public memory of that presidency. Toward that end, during his later years, Bancroft promulgated an anecdote in which Polk—as president elect or early during his presidency, versions vary—lists his presidential goals. Soon repeated in books by other historians, the story came to define Polk's presidency. (Library of Congress)

Historian James Schouler (1839–1920). In 1889, Schouler, in his *History of the United States of America, under the Constitution,* became the first historian to publish Bancroft's "four measures" anecdote concerning Polk. As Schouler indicated in a footnote, he learned the story from a February 1887 letter from Bancroft. (Library of Congress)

Historian Arthur Schlesinger Sr. In 1948, Schlesinger (1888-1965), in a survey, asked historians of the United States to rank all U.S. presidents by their performance in office. When their responses were averaged, Polk finished in tenth place. "Polk set himself certain precise objectives to be achieved while he was President, and achieve them he did," wrote Schlesinger approvingly. When Schlesinger repeated the exercise in 1962, Polk fared even better, finishing eighth. When his son, historian Arthur M. Schlesinger Jr., repeated the survey in 1996, Polk finished at number nine. (Massachusetts Historical Society)

Two later presidents, above, Theodore Roosevelt (1858–1919), and, below, Harry S. Truman (1884–1972), held starkly different views of Polk's presidency. To Roosevelt (circa 1904 photograph), Polk's expansionist triumphs resulted, in part, from his being bullied by slave powers into actions that produced problems left for later presidents to solve. Inveighed Roosevelt, Polk's "administration was neither capable nor warlike, however well disposed to bluster." Truman (ca. 1945 photograph), by contrast, rated Polk as "a great President." By Truman's lights, Polk "Said what he intended to do and did it." (Both photographs, Library of Congress)

Major League slugger Babe Ruth (1895–1948) in a circa 1921 photo. Allegedly, during the fifth inning of game three in the 1932 World Series, Ruth, while at bat and playing for the New York Yankees, made a pointing gesture to the center-field bleachers; he then proceeded, off the next pitch, to slam a home-run. Repeated ad infinitum in U.S. history textbooks, James Polk's alleged enumeration of his administration's "four great measures" has become U.S. political history's equivalent of Ruth's "called shot" of 1932. But, like Polk's alleged listing of goals, the legend of Babe's called home run comes fraught with a dubious provenance. According to one recent Ruth biographer, while some believe the story, evidence supporting it remains, at best inconclusive; among most experts, he writes, the story by now stands "debunked, seen as pure fable." (Library of Congress)

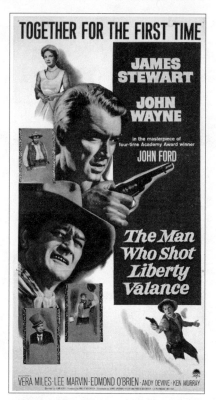

A poster for director John Ford's 1962 film, *The Man Who Shot Liberty Valance.* Known for films that explore the Old West and its legends, Ford (1893–1973) directed, during his half-century career, over 140 movies. *The Man Who Shot Liberty Valance* includes a scene that offers poetic insight into how a spurious anecdote—such as George Bancroft's story of Polk's early recitation of presidential goals—might find its way into the realm of accepted fact, and into history books: a veteran small-town newspaper editor is preparing a story on the killing of a gun-slinging outlaw who has long tormented the frontier community. Around town, credit—and attendant glory—for the killing has gone to the wrong man. The editor has recently learned the true killer's identity and is asked if a story he is about to publish will correct the error. "No, sir," he answers. "This is the West, sir. When the legend becomes fact, print the legend." (Margaret Herrick Library, at the Academy of Motion Picture Arts & Sciences; © Paramount Pictures Corp. All Rights Reserved.)

5

THE LEGENDS OF
MANIFEST DESTINY

Caveats against it notwithstanding, since Bancroft first recounted Polk's alleged enunciation, the bold pronouncement of goals has entered presidential lore. Repeated ad infinitum in U.S. history textbooks, it has become U.S. political history's equivalent of Babe Ruth's called home run of the 1932 World Series, in which the slugger allegedly gestured toward the outfield and, on the next pitch, slammed a home run. But then again, even the story of Ruth's "called shot" its appeal notwithstanding, rests on inconclusive evidence.[1]

Of course, a negative cannot be proven, and more credible evidence supporting the Polk anecdote may yet be located. But given the astonishing powers of presidential prescience depicted, it begs credulity to believe that other contemporaries—Polk himself, his friends and family, and other advisors—would not have recounted the incident early on, widely and frequently. But again, we know of no contemporary letter in which the anecdote appears. Nor does it appear in any of three Polk eulogies surveyed by this historian, tributes penned by prominent citizens and published in the wake of his death.[2]

Likewise, the anecdote makes no appearance in the first full accounts of, respectively, Polk's administration and his life—Lucien B. Chase's *History of the Polk Administration* and John S. Jenkins's *Life of James Knox Polk,* both generally adulatory and published in 1850.[3] Nor, for that matter, as noted above, does Bancroft himself recount the incident in the article on Polk that he wrote for *Appletons' Cyclopædia.*

The anecdote's origin and its insinuation into accepted history evoke an exchange from director John Ford's morality tale of the Old West, the 1962 film *The Man Who Shot Liberty Valance.* A veteran small-town newspaper editor is preparing a story on the killing of a gunslinging outlaw who has long tormented the frontier community. Around town, credit—and attendant glory—for the killing has gone to the wrong man. The editor has recently learned the true killer's identity and is asked if the story he is about to publish will correct the error. "No, sir," he answers. "This is the West, sir. When the legend becomes fact, print the legend."[4]

Over the years, Bancroft's legend has become "fact," and many historians have printed it. To be sure, Polk did accomplish the four objectives the anecdote enumerates. That cannot be denied. Nor can the magnitude of his achievement in increasing the nation's geographic size by a third. The point here is neither to diminish nor exalt Polk's presidency. Indeed, even without the anecdote's theatrics, a case, equally potent, could still be made for Polk as a shrewdly transformative president—one whose political acumen increased not only the size of the country but also the powers of the executive branch. Coincidentally, but in retrospect appropriately, it was during Polk's administration that an old British tune—soon known as "Hail to the Chief"—became a fixture of presidential protocol.[5]

Emblematic of Polk's presidential daring was the aplomb with which he essentially usurped the right, mandated by the U.S. Constitution, of Congress to declare war. As Polk biographer Walter R. Borneman observed, President James Madison, in seeking a war declaration from Congress for what became known as the War of 1812, was, as the Constitution's architect, keenly aware of that document's separation-of-powers doctrine and the executive branch's limits within that arrangement. Madison thus agonized over the war declaration and acceded to weeks of congressional debate before its passage.

By contrast, in May 1846 Polk aggressively petitioned Congress for a war measure against Mexico with a bellicose message that presented the conflict as a fait accompli: "the two nations are now at war." The House approved the war measure after but two hours of debate; the Senate took a day longer. Similarly, in prosecuting the subsequent conflict, Polk displayed a level of presidential involvement in war policies, then unprecedented in U.S. history, that would not be seen again until the administrations of Abraham Lincoln and Franklin Roosevelt.[6]

The point is that the Bancroft anecdote, factual or not, has had the effect of narrowing the scope of scrutiny accorded Polk's presidency—in effect allowing Polk (or Bancroft) to list and limit the events and objectives (the "measures") by which that presidency should be evaluated. To wit, even when Polk's actions have been criticized by historians, evaluations, favorable and otherwise, have tended to focus on the anecdote's four enumerated objectives.

Bancroft's list seemingly clarifies Polk's legacy. In practice, however, as deployed by historians, the anecdote obscures that legacy. Put another way, the story has become a restrictive, organizing principle for assessing Polk's term in office. Through its implicit endorsement of the meeting of set goals as a presidency's lone measure of success (Bancroft's "standpoint of results"), the anecdote has led historians to limit the scope of their assessment of Polk's term in office. Indeed, by their preoccupation with the goals enumerated in Bancroft's anecdote, historians have eschewed other yardsticks—moral, long range, or both—that might have yielded deeper, broader, and more thoughtful assessments. Beyond that, by focusing on the finite goals enunciated in Bancroft's ex post facto anecdote, historians have often tended to neglect other, lesser-known and less successful, domestic and foreign-policy initiatives of Polk's administration, as well as moments of confusion and indecision that eventually led to triumphs.

Begin with the Mexican War. Yes, Polk had forsworn a second term. But the war had barely begun when he came to suspect—wisely as it turned out—his two chief generals, the Whigs Zachary Taylor and Winfield Scott, of harboring presidential ambitions.[7] That wariness increasingly led Polk, already possessed of autocratic tendencies, toward involvement in war-related matters of strategy and personnel usually eschewed by civilian officials and left to military leaders.[8] A case in point: Polk's unsuccessful effort, documented in recently published correspondence, to install his ally Senator Thomas H. Benton as commanding general, outranking Scott and Taylor. Correspondence from that episode is at once fascinating reading and a cautionary tale of political hubris.[9]

By the summer of 1847, as Polk began his quest for a diplomatic end to the war in Mexico, the usual chess master had faltered. Having begun the war by arrogating duties usually tended by generals and cabinets officers, Polk became increasingly reliant on a retinue of secret agents he successively dispatched to Mexico in hopes of finding Mexican officials willing—and vested with requisite authority—to negotiate an armistice. Moreover, the correspondence suggests that as the conflict entered its endgame, no grand start-to-finish vision informed Polk's war strategy. Among questions to be resolved: How much of Mexico did the United States truly want to possess? And if, in resolving that question, the administration heeded the counsel of the "All Mexico" faction among congressional Democrats, what would be the consequences? What, Polk and others asked, would be the ramifications for the United States—militarily, politically, economically, and culturally—of occupying the entirety of Mexico? In the end, Polk—despite having dispatched orders for the dismissal of his final envoy, Nicholas P. Trist—accepted the armistice arranged by the diplomat. Trist's negotiations had won most of Polk's terms, and given the confusion that by then enveloped Mexico's government, the administration seemed unlikely to find, in the immediate future, other negotiating partners. Beyond that, Polk realized that continued congressional support for the war was far from certain.

As had Benjamin Franklin, Thomas Jefferson, John Quincy Adams, and other U.S. leaders before them, Polk allies such as Thomas H. Benton and George Bancroft elaborated overarching theories of history and empires.[10] But Polk himself declined lofty theorizing. Mostly—building on a longstanding, occasionally bipartisan, however intermittent, tradition of national territorial expansion—he saw opportunities. And if he judged them practical, he plunged ahead. Practical politics, not abstract philosophy, was Polk's métier.

Recently published letters document such tendencies. In 1847, as spring gave way to summer, the administration was looking beyond preoccupations with Mexico and Oregon. Letters from that period hint at broader and often-overlooked U.S. expansionist interests under Polk and his associates—concerns that go unmentioned in the Bancroft anecdote—such as Hawaii, Cuba, and other Latin American climes. Likewise, the correspondence reveals the administration's lively interest in European and British affairs, including Polk's personal interest in Ireland and the famine then ravaging the island. In March 1847, he placed two U.S. Navy ships into civilian hands to transport to Ireland foodstuffs donated by private charities.

Two years later, in the wake of the arrest, in Ireland, of John Mitchel and other Irish nationalists for planning a revolt intended to sunder the island from the United Kingdom, Polk instructed secretary of state Buchanan to have a communiqué sent to British officials requesting a pardon for the insurgents "who had recently attempted by a revolution to free themselves of the oppressions of their Government." The planned revolution had been easily thwarted, and Mitchel and others, soon convicted of felony sedition, were banished to a penal colony in today's Tasmania.[11] Beyond those concerns, the correspondence reveals the entwinement of Polk's direction of the Mexican War with concerns over party politics and other domestic political matters. Letters concerning upcoming political races show Polk and his far-flung supporters keeping a wary eye on Democratic fortunes across the country, from the upcoming 1848 presidential race to elections for state houses and the Congress. Beyond matters to be decided by voters, discussions of political patronage appointments— from local postmasterships to diplomatic postings and customs-house jobs—also won his attention. The letters reveal a party leader determined to use the spoils of office to reward allies and to deny political opponents, Whig and Democratic, berths in the federal bureaucracy.[12]

Ironically, this intensely private man bequeathed to posterity one of the most vivid accounts ever left by a U.S. president of his time in office. That circumstance owes less to any commitment to transparency than to happenstance. When Polk left Washington in March 1849, he anticipated passing his remaining years in Tennessee much as had his idol Andrew Jackson—as a revered, long-surviving elder statesman of the Democratic party. Newly published correspondence details the purchase of and renovation plans for the Nashville mansion in which Polk expected to spend those postpresidency years.[13] Untimely death, however, likely from cholera, three months after leaving the presidency, denied Polk that long retirement. (Indeed, it marked the briefest postpresidency retirement in U.S. history.) That early demise also denied Polk the opportunity to destroy or edit the diary he had kept for most of his presidency—a diary eventually published in 1910.

Likewise, his untimely death denied Polk the opportunity to select the letters that eventually found their way into various archives. That circumstance increases the level of candor that informs much of Polk's correspondence. And unlike other presidents, he left behind no offspring to cull the letters—to decide which to destroy and which to preserve for posterity—most of which have only recently been published for the first time, or, if current plans proceed, will be published in the near future.

Yet another irony of Polk's legacy—again, highlighted by recently published correspondence—concerns the role historians have assigned him in fostering sectionalism. In 1846, Ralph Waldo Emerson warned, "The United States will conquer Mexico, but it will be as the man swallows the arsenic, which brings him down in turn. Mexico will poison us."[14] By now, many, perhaps most, historians have accepted the prescience of Emerson's warning. They agree that Polk's 1846–48 war in Mexico exacerbated North-South sectional tensions that, in the intervening years, led to the secession crisis of 1860–61 and the American Civil War of 1861–65. But that view, however valid, obscures how Polk and his supporters viewed themselves in the world as they found it.

The correspondence, much of it concerning the business affairs of his two plantations, documents Polk the private businessman, intimately involved in the buying and selling of slaves. Polk harbored reservations concerning the moral efficacy of slavery. As a planter and businessman, however, he seldom acted on those qualms.[15] By contrast with that acquiescence to the institution of slavery, Polk, nominally a Presbyterian—not until close to death was he baptized—and a descendant of seventeenth-century Protestant emigrants from Ireland's province of Ulster to the United States, displayed a principled distaste for anti-Catholic bigotry and, as president, acted upon that conviction.[16]

But while Polk made no effort to hide the fact that he was a slaveholder, he did seek to conceal from the public the details of those business affairs, as well as the amount of time he spent during his presidency dealing with slave trading. In a postscript to an 1847 letter to a Tennessee plantation manager, he warns,

> I need scarcely repeat to you my former request that as my *private business* does not concern the public, you will keep it to yourself. There is a great disposition with many persons, to parade every thing connected with the President whether *private or not* before the public. This I do not desire shall be the case. *Majr. Childress* explained to you last year the propriety of this suggestion; & I repeat it now, but possibly you might not appreciate its importance. J. K. P.[17]

Necessity obliged Polk to sustain Democratic party support—to keep political fences mended—on both sides of the Mason-Dixon line. Thus, as much as possible, he sought to avoid growing North-South sectional tensions over slavery. More to the point, like his mentor Andrew Jackson, he strived to present himself as the quintessential Unionist.

By Polk's lights, dangers to national unity came primarily not from southern slaveholders but from New England opponents of the South's slavery. From his vantage, the latter were challenging what he and his southern allies defended as an institution sanctioned by custom and the U.S. Constitution. Polk and other Democrats often repeated the charge that it had been not southern slaveholders but New England Federalists, forerunners of the Whigs, who had introduced the threat of secession into American politics. A motion to break away from the Union had been associated with the Hartford Convention, convened by New England Federalists to oppose the War of 1812. Hence, in 1847, a navy officer and political supporter took time off from war duty to warn President Polk, "In the Navy we have a great majority of federalists—old federalists of the Hartford Convention stamp who would like, honestly, to see the Union dissolved."[18]

Indeed, underscoring Polk's commitment to national unity, among his first acts after becoming president was to have the Democratic party's Washington organ placed under new ownership and its name changed from the *Washington Globe* to the *Washington Union.*

Truth be known, James K. Polk harbored no particular intellectual curiosity about the then barely mapped western topographies of California, Oregon, and the Southwest—realms that he had dispatched John Frémont to explore and that Polk ultimately brought under U.S. dominion. Alas, one can only speculate how the fact that the president had never seen a desert—much less understood the problems faced by his armies in Mexico crossing such landscapes—shaped his early optimism concerning the Mexican War. A May 1846 diary entry captured that sanguine spirit; recounting a conversation with Senator Benton from earlier that day, Polk noted that he had expressed his belief that "with a large force on land and sea I thought it [the war] could be easily terminated."[19]

Tellingly, as president-elect in 1845, Polk had given short shrift to Frémont, freshly returned from the second of the three federally sponsored western expeditions that he led. Polk was dismissive when the explorer said that he knew from firsthand experience that major rivers indicated on a map before them were misrepresented. One, Frémont said—the Buenaventura, reputed to be the Mississippi of the West—did not even exist. The explorer recalled that the president-elect "found me 'young' and said something of the 'impulsiveness of young men,' and was not at all satisfied in his own mind that those rivers were not running there as laid down."[20]

Even so, to the degree that regional identity animated the president, he seems to have thought himself as much, perhaps more, a man of the West as of the South—though decidedly not Frémont's West. In a May 21, 1847, letter, Polk recalls having moved as a child from his North Carolina birthplace to "the West"—the town of Columbia, Tennessee, south of Nashville.[21] As a successful young trial lawyer during the 1830s, Polk acquired a plantation in Columbia and soon extended his land holdings westward, purchasing properties in Arkansas, western Tennessee, and Mississippi. Perhaps, then, the phrase that best locates Polk's regional orientation—actual and by ambition—is the "Old Southwest," a term of that era that referred to regions west of the Appalachians, east of the Mississippi, and south of the Ohio River. And, in the end, that the task of culminating America's long march to the Pacific—and its emergence as a coast-to-coast, continental nation-state— fell to a man of such modest personal horizons certainly numbers among the many ironies of the public career of James K. Polk.

THE ROAD TO FORT SUMTER

In politics, as in business and comedy, timing can be everything. And luck too never hurts. By now James K. Polk's name is entwined with the places that he is credited with adding to Old Glory's dominion—Texas, the Pacific Northwest, the arid Southwest, and California. The fact that the eleventh president's intention of acquiring Cuba was sabotaged by an ill-timed disclosure by James Gordon Bennett's *New York Herald* is by now little remembered. Neither are the missteps and lucky breaks that attended Polk on the way to his expansionist successes.

In the summer of 1846, for instance, the Polk administration dispatched U.S. naval officer Alexander Slidell Mackenzie to travel as a special messenger to Havana, Cuba, to meet with the exiled former ruler of Mexico, General Antonio López de Santa Anna. Mackenzie carried an order from Navy Secretary George Bancroft for the navy to permit Santa Anna to return to his native land. In exchange for facilitating his return to power, Santa Anna agreed to, once back in power, extend to the United States peace and territorial concessions. Santa Anna returned to Mexico that August—but he did not uphold the agreement.

When, however, congressional Whigs lambasted Polk's actions and demanded to see the paper trail that had led to the deception, Polk refused to submit records of Mackenzie's meetings. Under other circumstances, the impasse might have yielded the sort of difficulties that befell President Ronald Reagan in 1986 during the Iran-Contra scandal. But Polk weathered the imbroglio, and another diplomat, the State Department's Nicholas Trist, secretly dispatched to Mexico in 1848, negotiated an armistice that ended the Mexican War and ultimately gained Polk's approval.[1]

More broadly, it also did not hurt Polk that many if not all of the expansionist initiatives that it fell to him to consummate had begun under earlier presidents, and indeed stretched back to the dawn of the American Republic. The United States—upon its founding as a loosely affiliated confederation of former British colonies on the Atlantic seaboard—had inherited from its mother country a quest for empire.

Britain's empire had been built on trade—powered by a mercantilist dynamic by which far-flung colonies enriched the metropolis—and had been outward looking and maritime in scope. By contrast, the American Republic, in its expansionist stirrings, came by the 1840s to embrace a notion of empire more inward looking and continental in scope—eventually preoccupied as much with settlement as with commerce. Acting on expansionist ambitions, predecessors of James Polk—presidents from Jefferson to Tyler —intermittently pursued diplomacy and wars: The 1803 Louisiana Purchase pushed American claims west of the Mississippi; the War of 1812, altering no boundaries, secured earlier U.S. claims west of the Appalachians; by the 1818 "joint occupation" agreement, the United States and the United Kingdom agreed officially, for the time being, to share the sprawling Oregon Country; and in 1819, the Adams-Onís Treaty between the United States and Spain secured Florida for the American domain and—establishing a template for later action—projected American power into parts of Texas and the Southwest.

Polk and Zachary Taylor, the first of his two successive chief generals in the Mexican theater, had, through messages and intermediaries, often quarreled. Discomfiting Polk was his suspicion that Taylor, a Whig, harbored postwar political ambitions. So after Taylor's election to the presidency in 1848—defeating Democrat and Polk ally Lewis Cass—it came as no surprise to anyone that the president and the president-elect did not share warm relations. But on the morning of March 5, 1849, during a shared carriage ride following Taylor's swearing-in ceremony, the men's mutual distaste for one another grew, on Polk's part, into outright incredulousness.

During the ride, Taylor essentially said that that the country's recent triumphs in the Far West had been for naught. According to Polk's diary, Taylor used the occasion to express his view that Oregon and California were "too distant to become members of the Union, and that it would be better for them to be an "Independant [*sic*] Gov[ern]ment." Even after the new president, for emphasis, repeated them, Polk "made no response" to Taylor's expressed views on California and Oregon. Even so, he found them "alarming opinions to be entertained by the President of the U.S."[2]

In voicing his reservations concerning Oregon's and California's lying too distant to ever become full partners in the American Union, Taylor was likely haunted by the American Whig party's traditional fears of the dangers that attend a too geographically dispersed Republic. As Massachusetts senator Daniel Webster—urging settlement of existing territories instead of the conquering of others—had warned during the heady days of 1840s expansionism, "You have a Sparta . . . embellish it!"[3] In his doubting, of course, Taylor failed to envision how the forces of commerce, settlement, and various technologies—including, most immediately, the railroad and the telegraph—would soon meld the country.

In the end, neither man would live to witness the Far West's integration into the Union. Polk would die three months after leaving the White House. And Taylor—succumbing to violent illness in 1850 after attending a July 4 celebration at the site of the newly dedicated but far from finished Washington Monument—would not live to complete his term as president. Moreover—reinforcing the sense that both belonged to a disappearing era—Polk and Taylor would be the final two U.S. presidents to own slaves during their term in office; and neither foresaw how the military victories each had played a role in winning would, within a dozen years, lead to a conflict that, countervailing all forces of national unity, violently divided the United States.

In the spring of 1847, as American forces waged war against Mexico, Polk, in a letter to one of his generals, had indulged a moment to contemplate better days. "In truth," he wrote Gideon Pillow, "the war is now the all-absorbing question of my administration." Even so, he allowed, the "country is prosperous in a degree almost without an example, and if the war can be brought to a successful termination, a long course of prosperity is before us, and I shall retire at the close of my term, with the satisfaction of believing I have rendered my country some service."[4] But the coming years did not redeem Polk's expectations. His retirement was cruelly brief, and the legacy of peace and prosperity that he envisioned for the country, which his policies had so enlarged, was also short lived. As president, his policies had perpetuated and expanded the domain of a mode of labor—human chattel slavery—already banned in much of the world. Those policies, in turn, exacerbated sectional divisions within the American Union. And, in the end, the eleventh president's territorial attainments—what some, but never Polk, celebrated as a fulfillment of the spirit of Manifest Destiny—inexorably led the nation toward its darkest hour.

NOTES

Introduction

1. Norman Mailer, *Conversations with Norman Mailer,* ed. J. Michael Lennon (Oxford: Univ. Press of Mississippi, 2008), 194.

2. James K. Polk, *Correspondence of James K. Polk: Volume XII, January–July 1847,* ed. Tom Chaffin and Michael David Cohen (Knoxville: Univ. of Tennessee Press, 2013); Tom Chaffin, "Mitt Romney: The Second Coming of James K. Polk?" *Atlantic.com,* Oct. 3, 2012, http://www.theatlantic.com/politics/archive/2012/10/mitt-romney-the-second-coming-of-james-k-polk/263018/; Nancy Forger to author, email, Oct. 8, 2012.

1. Traces of the Dark Horse

1. For "I took the chair," see Dec. 5, 1848 entry, in "George Mifflin Dallas Diary, 1848-1849" [photocopy of original], Historical Society of Pennsylvania, Philadelphia. Rounding out the borders of today's continental United States, President Franklin Pierce, in 1854, purchased from Mexico a thirty-thousand-square-mile area in what is now the states of Arizona and New Mexico. The transaction, known as the Gadsden Purchase, takes its name from James Gadsden, then U.S. minister to Mexico. "It is geography," from Robert D. Kaplan, *The Revenge of Geography: What the Map Tells Us About Coming Conflicts and the Battle Against Fate* (New York: Random House, 2012), 32–33.

2. "Joint occupation," by which the United States and the United Kingdom agreed to defer disputes over their respective claims to lands in the Oregon Country, was established by the Treaty of 1818. The two countries renewed the arrangement in 1826,

with the stipulation that if either sought to abrogate joint occupation, each would give the other one year's notice before doing so. Mexico's title to New Mexico, Texas, and California—all former colonies of Spain—had been established, in 1821, by Mexico's victory over Spain in the Mexican War of Independence (1810–21).

3. The place Americans know as California was called Alta California by successive Spanish and Mexican officials. The appellation distinguished it from Baja California Sur, today a state in Mexico's federal union. In this volume, "Alta California" and "California" appear as synonyms. Immediately prior to and during the Mexican War, the governance and administrative divisions of the Republic of Mexico underwent frequent changes. Between 1836 and 1846—the period of the Centralist Republic—the country was divided into departments. For governance of Mexico's north during the era, see David J. Weber, *The Mexican Frontier, 1821–1846: The American Southwest under Mexico* (Albuquerque: Univ. of New Mexico Press, 1982).

4. George Pierce Garrison, *Westward Extension, 1841–1850* (New York: Harper & Brothers, 1906), 207.

5. Frank del Olmo, "Line Drawn in 1848 Shaped Who We Are," *Los Angeles Times,* March 1, 1998.

6. For Polk's formal education, see Charles Sellers, *James K. Polk: Jacksonian, 1795–1843* (Princeton, N.J.: Princeton Univ. Press, 1957), 41–55.

7. Abolitionist James G. Birney, representing the Liberty party, was also a presidential candidate in 1844. Although Birney won but 2.3 percent of the popular vote, many scholars believe that his candidacy, attracting antislavery votes that otherwise would have gone to Clay, threw the election to Polk. For Birney's role in Polk's victory, see Paul H. Bergeron, *The Presidency of James K. Polk* (Lawrence: Univ. Press of Kansas, 1987), 19–20; and Charles Sellers, *James K. Polk: Continentalist, 1843–1846* (Princeton, N.J.: Princeton Univ. Press, 1966), 156.

8. The U.S. war with Mexico (1846–48) has been accorded many names. In this work, I call it what Polk called it—the Mexican

War. For astute military studies of the war from a U.S. perspective, see K. Jack Bauer, *The Mexican War, 1846–1848* (New York: Macmillan, 1974); and Richard Bruce Winders, *Mr. Polk's Army: The American Military Experience in the Mexican War* (College Station: Texas A&M Univ. Press, 1997). For more recent accounts of the war, focused on domestic debates over the conflict rather than events in the war theater, see Amy S. Greenberg, *A Wicked War: Polk, Clay, Lincoln and the 1846 U.S. Invasion of Mexico* (New York: Alfred A. Knopf, 2012); and Robert W. Merry, *A Country of Vast Designs: James K. Polk, the Mexican War and the Conquest of the American Continent* (New York: Simon & Schuster, 2009). For other recent studies of Polk, see Thomas M. Leonard, *James Polk: A Clear and Unquestionable Destiny*, Biographies in American Foreign Policy series (Lanham, Md.: Rowman & Littlefield, 2000); and John Seigenthaler, *James K. Polk*, American Presidents series (New York: Times Books, 2003). Most military histories of the Mexican War give short shrift to the conflict's California theater. For a splendid exception to that tendency, see Neal Harlow, *California Conquered: The Annexation of a Mexican Province, 1846–1850* (Berkeley and Los Angeles: Univ. of California Press, 1982).

9. For reference to the Battle of Palo Alto (near the mouth of the Rio Grande) in Polk's correspondence, see Polk to Zachary Taylor, May 30, 1846, in James K. Polk, *Correspondence of James K. Polk: Volume XI, 1846,* ed. Wayne Cutler (Knoxville: Univ. of Tennessee Press, 2009), 188; for Resaca del Palma, see John W. Mason to Polk, Oct. 27, 1846, Polk, *Correspondence* 11:367–69; for Santa Fe (New Mexico), see William H. Polk to Polk, Oct. 6, 1846, Polk, *Correspondence* 11:336–38; for Monterey (California), see Polk to Thomas H. Benton, Sept. 1, 1846, Polk, *Correspondence* 11:299; for Monterrey (eastern Mexico), see Robert M. McLane to Polk, Dec. 12, 1846, Polk, *Correspondence* 11:411–13; for Buena Vista, see John M. Patton to Polk, [Mar. 30, 1847], Polk, *Correspondence* 12:161–62; for Sacramento (in Chihuahua, Mexico), see Polk to Robert Armstrong, May 13, 1847, Polk, *Correspondence* 12:245; for Veracruz, see Jeremiah George Harris to Polk, Mar. 29, 1847, Polk, *Correspondence* 12:154–55; for

Cerro Gordo, see Henry C. Pope, May 1, 1847, Polk, *Correspondence* 12:219–21.

10. For letters pertaining to the capture and subsequent occupation of Mexico City, see William O. Butler to Polk, Sept. 11, 1847, and Polk to Aaron V. Brown, Oct. 18, 1847, both in James K. Polk Papers, Manuscript Division, Library of Congress, Washington, D.C. (hereafter cited as Polk Papers).

11. For but one example of July 1847 discussions regarding U.S. territorial spoils from the war, see Anthony W. Butler to Polk, July 16, 1847, Polk, *Correspondence*, 12: 424-26; in the missive, Butler advocates U.S. acquisition of Mexico's Isthmus of Tehuantepec, long considered a propitious location for an Atlantic-to-Pacific canal. By the eventual peace terms, however, Mexico kept the isthmus; see Anthony W. Butler to Polk, July 16, 1847, Polk, *Correspondence* 12:424–26. More broadly, among other justifications that Polk and his allies invoked for their actions in Texas and Oregon was that both areas, by prior rights, belonged to the United States. The 1844 Democratic party platform thus spoke of the "reoccupation" of Oregon and the "re-annexation of Texas." From their vantage, the U.S. claim to Oregon stretched back to explorations, in 1792, of the Columbia River's lower reaches by U.S. merchant and sea captain Robert Gray, as well as subsequent, early U.S. activity along the Pacific Northwest Coast. That U.S. claim, Polk and his allies argued, had been improperly surrendered by the Anglo-U.S. Treaty of 1818. Similarly, regarding Texas, Polk and his allies maintained that the Louisiana Purchase (1803) had included Texas but the Adams-Onís Treaty (1819) between the United States and Spain had improperly transferred Texas to Spain.

2. The Expansionist

1. Polk, "First Annual Message," Dec. 2, 1845, in *A Compilation of the Messages and Papers of the Presidents, 1789–1897,* ed. James D. Richardson (Washington, D.C.: GPO, 1897), 4:398; entry of Oct. 24, 1845, in James K. Polk, *The Diary of James K. Polk during His Presidency, 1845 to 1849,* 4 vols., ed. Milo Milton

Quaife (Chicago: A. C. McClurg, 1910) (hereafter cited as Polk, *Diary,* followed by the volume and page number), 1:70. For a discussion of Polk and the Monroe Doctrine, see Jay Sexton, *The Monroe Doctrine: Empire and Nation in Nineteenth-Century America* (New York: Hill & Wang, 2011), 97–118.

2. Eric Foner, *Politics and Ideology in the Age of the Civil War* (New York: Oxford Univ. Press, 1981), 84.

3. Frederick Douglass lecture, Sunderland, England, Sept. 18, 1846, in Frederick Douglass, *The Frederick Douglass Papers,* ser. 1, *Speeches, Debates, and Interviews,* vol. 1, ed. John W. Blassingame (New Haven, Conn.: Yale Univ. Press, 1979), 419.

4. The Treaty of Guadalupe Hidalgo stipulated that, in exchange for abandoning claims to Texas, New Mexico, and California, the Mexican government would be paid fifteen million dollars by the United States. The U.S. government also agreed to pay Mexican debts, relieving Mexico's government of about five million dollars in claims against it by U.S. citizens. The treaty also, in general terms, stipulated anew the boundary between the two nations, with clarifications to be made by a joint U.S.-Mexico commission.

5. For Polk's abstemious habits, see Mark E. Byrnes, *James K. Polk: A Biographical Companion* (Santa Barbara, Calif.: ABC-CLIO, 2001), 171; Polk to Bancroft, Jan. 30, 1847, Polk, *Correspondence* 12:65–66.

6. John L. O'Sullivan, "Annexation," *United States Magazine and Democratic Review* 17 (July–Aug. 1845): 5; Robert D. Sampson, *John L. O'Sullivan and His Times* (Kent, Ohio: Kent State Univ. Press, 2003), 193–207.

7. Walter R. Borneman, *Polk: The Man Who Transformed the Presidency and America* (New York: Random House, 2008), 219.

8. Tom Chaffin, *Fatal Glory: Narciso López and the First Clandestine U.S. War against Cuba* (Charlottesville: Univ. Press of Virginia, 1996; reprint, Baton Rouge: Louisiana State Univ. Press, 2003), 18. For more on U.S. interest in Cuba and on filibusters—clandestine armies, usually from the United States, bent on conquests in foreign, often Latin American, climes—see

both Chaffin, *Fatal Glory,* and Robert E. May, *Manifest Destiny's Underworld: Filibustering in Antebellum America* (Chapel Hill: Univ. of North Carolina Press, 2001).

9. For "All Mexico," see Frederick Merk, *Manifest Destiny and Mission in American History* (1963; reprint, Cambridge: Harvard Univ. Press, 1995), 112–13; for Cuba, see Chaffin, *Fatal Glory,* 14–15, 35–36, 41–43; for "expressed no opinion," see entry of May 10, 1848, Polk, *Diary* 3:446. For Saunders, see Chaffin, *Fatal Glory,* 41–43.

10. Walt Whitman, "Song of Myself" (1855), in *Walt Whitman: Complete Poetry and Collected Prose,* ed. Justin Kaplan (New York: Library of America, 1982), 59; Henry David Thoreau, "Walking," in *Henry David Thoreau: Collected Essays and Poems,* ed. Elizabeth Hall Witherell (New York: Library of America, 2001), 234.

11. Entry for May 31, 1847, in Polk, *Diary* 3:45.

12. On Polk's "Napoleon of the Stump" accolade and speaking style, see John S. Jenkins, *The Life of James Knox Polk: Late President of the United States* (Auburn, N.Y.: James M. Alden, 1850), 50–51; see also Sellers, *Polk: Jacksonian,* 275–78. Neither work, however, cites a contemporary usage—a usage during Polk's lifetime—of that epithet.

13. Sellers, *Polk: Continentalist,* 307.

14. For visits by nieces and nephews, see Robert Armstrong to Polk, Jan. 4, 1847, *Correspondence* 12:26; and Polk to Sarah Childress Polk, July 11, 1847, *Correspondence* 12:417.

15. Thomas Hart Benton, *Thirty Years' View; or, A History of the Working of the American Government for Thirty Years, from 1820 to 1850,* vol. 2 (New York: D. Appleton, 1883), 680.

16. For "mischievous" remark, see entry of Aug. 10, 1846, Polk, *Diary* 2:75; for California, Oregon, and Calhoun, see entry of Apr. 6, 1847, Polk, *Diary* 2:457–59.

17. Chaffin, *Fatal Glory,* 26–30; Merk, *Manifest Destiny and Mission,* 61–64.

3. The Autocrat

1. Tom Chaffin, *Pathfinder: John Charles Frémont and the Course of American Empire* (New York: Hill & Wang, 2002), 82–85, 146, 181, 252–53, 272, 307, 389–408, 415–17, 423–30, 490–92. When Nicollet died in 1843, Frémont was promoted to fill the leadership role, formerly held by Nicollet, in subsequent surveys of the region. For Jefferson's planning of Lewis and Clark expedition, see James P. Ronda, *Lewis & Clark among the Indians* (Lincoln: University of Nebraska Press, 1984), 1–8.

2. Polk to Cornelius W. Lawrence, May 24, 1847, Polk, *Correspondence* 12:289–90.

3. Norman Gash, *Sir Robert Peel: The Life of Sir Robert Peel after 1830* (London: Longman, 1972), 527–30.

4. Entry of Dec. 29, 1848, Polk, *Diary* 4:261. For Polk's work habits, see also Sellers, *Polk: Continentalist,* 301–6, and Eugene Irving McCormac, *James K. Polk: A Political Biography* (Berkeley and Los Angeles: Univ. of California Press, 1922), 328–29.

5. For telegraph report of 1844 nomination, see Donald Ritchie, *Press Gallery: Congress and the Washington Correspondents* (Cambridge, Mass: Harvard University Press, 1993), 30. For first photographic portrait in White House, see Clifford Krainik, "A 'Dark Horse' in Sunlight and Shadow: Daguerreotypes of President James K. Polk," *White House History* 2, no. 1 (June 1997), 44. For first postage stamp, see John Nicholas Luff, *The Postage Stamps of the United States* (N.Y: Scott Stamp and Coin Co., 1902), 62.

4. The Historian and the President

1. Lilian Handlin, *George Bancroft: The Intellectual as Democrat* (New York: Harper and Row, 1984), 208–10. Bancroft, "Biographical Sketch of James K. Polk," typescript, c. late 1880s, p. 25, repeated with slight variation on p. 2 (the second of two pages numbered as p. 2), George Bancroft Papers, Manuscript and Archives Division, New York Public Library; George Bancroft to James Grant Wilson, Mar. 8, 1888, quoted in an addendum

to George Bancroft, "Polk, James K.," in *Appletons' Cyclopædia of American Biography,* ed. James Grant Wilson and John Fiske (New York: D. Appleton, 1888), 5:55. In a magazine article, an aging John Frémont presents a letter from the same period in which Bancroft recounts the same anecdote. Bancroft to Frémont, Sept. 2, 1886, quoted in John Frémont, "The Conquest of California," *Century Illustrated Magazine* 41 (Apr. 1891): 923.

2. James Schouler, *History of the United States of America, under the Constitution,* vol. 4, *1831–1847* (Washington, D.C.: William H. Morrison, 1889), 498. See also George Bancroft to Schouler, Feb. 5, 1887, in James Schouler Autograph Collection, Massachusetts Historical Society, Boston.

3. McCormac, *James K. Polk,* 351, 725.

4. Arthur M. Schlesinger, "Historians Rate the U.S. Presidents," *Life,* Nov. 1, 1948, 65–66; Arthur M. Schlesinger, "Our Presidents: A Rating by 75 Historians," *New York Times Magazine,* July 29, 1962, 12, 41; Arthur M. Schlesinger Jr., "Rating the Presidents: Washington to Clinton," *Political Science Quarterly* 112 (Summer 1997): 179, 181, 183, 189.

5. Harry S. Truman to Dean Acheson, Aug. 26, 1960 (version not sent), in Harry S. Truman, *Affection and Trust: The Personal Correspondence of Harry S. Truman and Dean Acheson, 1953–1971,* ed. Ray Geselbracht (New York: Alfred A. Knopf, 2010), 246. Asked, on another occasion, for his personal list of greatest presidents, Truman ranked Washington first, Jefferson second, Jackson third; "then James K. Polk, who expanded the country to the Pacific and gave us space as a continental power and a chance to grow into one of the greatest republics. James K. Polk paid the same price for that part of the country that Thomas Jefferson paid for Louisiana. Don't forget that." Harry S. Truman, *Truman Speaks* (New York: Columbia Univ. Press, 1960), 24.

6. Jon Ward, "The One-Termer?" *Huffington Post,* Aug. 21, 2012, http://www.huffingtonpost.com/2012/08/21/the-one-termer_n_1819608.html/.

7. For just two examples of the four goals in textbooks, see George Brown Tindall with David E. Shi, *America: A Narrative His-*

tory, 3rd ed. (New York: W. W. Norton, 1984), 540; and Joseph R. Conlin, *The American Past: A Survey of American History,* vol. 1, *To 1877,* 9th ed. (Boston: Wadsworth, Cengage Learning, 2012), 389. The indie rock group They Might Be Giants gained attention with its 1996 recording of "James K. Polk," a spritely song that offered a mock celebration of Polk's presidency, with lyrics recounting his alleged objectives and attainment of them ("In four short years he met his every goal").

8. Polk to Marcy, May 9, 1849, in William L. Marcy Papers, Manuscript Division, Library of Congress. For further details on Marcy as a prospective biographer, see John McDonough, "History of the Collection," in *James K. Polk Papers: A Finding Aid to the Collection in the Library of Congress,* rev. ed. (Washington, D.C.: Manuscript Division, Library of Congress, 2010), 8.

9. Theodore Roosevelt, *Life of Thomas Hart Benton* (Boston: Houghton Mifflin, 1886), 287, 311–13, 328.

10. McCormac, *James K. Polk,* v, 724.

11. Frederick Jackson Turner, "The Significance of the Frontier in American History," *Proceedings of the State Historical Society of Wisconsin* 41 (1894): 104, 106, 108–9. For Benton as "man as widest views," see Turner, "Significance of the Frontier," 109.

12. For Bancroft and Bismarck, see Handlin, *Bancroft,* 300–310. See also Russel B. Nye, *George Bancroft: Brahmin Rebel* (New York: Alfred K. Knopf, 1945), 241–61. Polk to Marcy, Nashville, May 9, 1849, Polk Papers. See also McDonough, "History of the Collection," 9–10—though he errs in stating year of Bancroft's Nashville visit.

13. For more on Polk's treatment by historians during the nineteenth century and into the early twentieth century, see McCormac, *James K. Polk,* 724–25; and Handlin, *Bancroft,* 340–41. Bancroft's earlier and other major biographer, Russel B. Nye, unlike Handlin, accepts the four-goals enunciation at face value. Nye, *Bancroft,* 137.

14. For "keeps his own counsels most closely," see George Bancroft to Elizabeth Davis Bancroft, Feb. 17, 1845, George Bancroft Papers, Division of Rare and Manuscript Collections, Cornell University Library. For Bancroft's waiting in Washington, in

February 1845, to learn what position he would hold in the new administration, see Handlin, *Bancroft,* 198–99. Of all the letters thus far encountered, the one that comes closest to confirming Bancroft's anecdote is one, located by my colleague Michael Cohen, that was enclosed in Edmund Burke to Polk, Oct. 9, 1847, Polk Papers. The enclosed letter, Nathaniel G. Upham to Edmund Burke, written September 28, 1847, includes the following: "A gentleman of some standing in Massachusetts, friendly to the President, remarked to me after the establishment of the new Tariff, the settlement of the Oregon question, & the movement on Mexico, 'that President Polk was desirous of doing every thing that would have to be done within the next fifty years.'" The Massachusetts gentleman is likely Bancroft, but the list includes no mention of California—the only one of Polk's territorial attainments not initiated by concrete policies of earlier administrations. And the letter's date, September 1847, comes deep into his term in office, far too late to indicate the president's prescience of his eventual accomplishments.

15. Mangum to Tod R. Caldwell, Feb. 20, 1845, in Willie Person Mangum, *Papers of Willie Person Mangum,* vol. 4, *1844–1846,* ed. Henry Thomas Shanks (Raleigh: North Carolina Department of Archives and History, 1955), 268. For external threats against Texas in early 1845, see Sellers, *Polk: Continentalist,* 215, 259–63; Borneman, *Polk,* 168, 178, 193–94; and Bergeron, *Presidency of James K. Polk,* 53, 60–61.

16. Entry of Oct. 24, 1845, Polk, *Diary* 1:71; Bancroft to Polk, Aug. 5, 1848, Bancroft Papers, Mass. Historical Society.

5. The Legends of Manifest Destiny

1. According to Ruth biographer Leigh Montville, while some believe the "called shot" story, evidence supporting it remains, at best, inconclusive. Among most experts, he contends, the story by now stands "debunked, seen as pure fable." Leigh Montville, *The Big Bam: The Life and Times of Babe Ruth* (New York: Random House, 2007), 310–12.

2. H. S. Foote, *Eulogy upon the Life and Character of James K. Polk, Late President of the United States, Delivered at Washington City, July 9, 1849* (Washington, D.C.: Thomas Ritchie, 1849).

3. Lucien B. Chase, *History of the Polk Administration* (New York: John F. Trow, 1850); Jenkins, *Life of James Knox Polk*.

4. *The Man Who Shot Liberty Valence*, dir. John Ford, 123 min., Paramount Pictures, Los Angeles, 1962.

5. For "Hail to the Chief," See Borneman, *Polk*, 144.

6. Polk, war message to Congress, May 11, 1846, in James D. Richardson, ed., *A Compilation of the Messages and Papers of the Presidents, 1789–1897* (Washington, D.C.: GPO, 1899), 9:437–43; Sellers, *Polk: Continentalist*, 265–66, 416–20; for a comparison of Polk with other presidents in wielding executive powers, see Borneman, *Polk*, 208–10.

7. Scott had sought the 1840 Whig presidential nomination, which ultimately went to William Henry Harrison.

8. John C. Pinheiro, *Manifest Ambition: James K. Polk and Civil-Military Relations during the Mexican War* (Westport, Conn.: Praeger Security International, 2007), 59–81, 134–40.

9. See, for instance, Benton to Polk, Mar. 6, 1847, Polk, *Correspondence* 12:111–13; Polk to Benton, Mar. 9, 1847, Polk, *Correspondence* 12:118; and Polk to Robert J. Armstrong, Apr. 28, 1847, Polk, *Correspondence* 12:204–6.

10. Richard W. Van Alstyne, *The Rising American Empire* (1960; reprint, New York: W. W. Norton, 1974), 1–27; Chaffin, *Pathfinder*, 7–18; on specifically Jefferson, see also Peter S. Onuf, *Jefferson's Empire: The Language of American Nationhood* (Charlottesville: Univ. Press of Virginia, 2000). For astute works on U.S. expansionism, slavery, the pursuit of American empire, and other themes, see also Norman A. Graebner, *Empire on the Pacific: A Study in Continental Expansion* (Claremont, Calif.: Regina Books, 1983); Reginald Horsman, *Race and Manifest Destiny: Origins of American Racial Anglo-Saxonism* (Cambridge: Harvard Univ. Press, 1981); Michael A. Morrison, *Slavery and the American West: The Eclipse of Manifest Destiny* (Chapel Hill: Univ.

of North Carolina Press, 1999); Gregory H. Nobles, *American Frontiers: Cultural Encounters and Continental Conquest* (New York: Hill and Wang, 1997; Walter Nugent, *Habits of Empire: A History of American Expansion* (New York: Alfred Knopf, 2008); David M. Pletcher, *The Diplomacy of Annexation: Texas, Oregon, and the Mexican War* (Columbia: Univ. of Missouri Press, 1973); Albert K. Weinberg, *Manifest Destiny: A Study of Nationalist Expansionism in American History* (Baltimore: Johns Hopkins Press, 1935).

11. For examples of interest in Hawaii, see Joel Turrill to Polk, Mar. 25, 1847, Polk, *Correspondence* 12:145–49; in Cuba, William R. King and James E. Saunders to Polk, May 29, 1847, Polk, *Correspondence* 12:308–10; in Brazil, John Y. Mason to Polk, Feb. 13, 1847, Polk, *Correspondence* 12: 84–85; in the Irish famine, Robert Gray to Polk, Feb. 22, 1847, Polk, *Correspondence* 12: 96–98; in European and British affairs, Bancroft to Polk, Jan. 4. 1847, Polk, *Correspondence* 12:28–31. For requested pardons for Mitchel and other Irish rebels, see entry of Sept. 5, 1848, Polk, *Diary*, 4:117–19.

12. For concerns with patronage and politics, see Polk to Gideon J. Pillow, Apr. 14, 1847, Polk, *Correspondence* 12:176–79; Polk to Caleb Cushing, Apr. 15, 1847, Polk, *Correspondence* 12:179–80; Polk to Daniel Graham, Apr. 26, 1847, Polk, *Correspondence* 12:200–201.

13. Among the many letters related to his post–presidency home, see Polk to John M. Bass, Apr. 19, 1847, Polk, *Correspondence* 12:184.

14. Journal entry of May or June 1846, Ralph Waldo Emerson, *Journals of Ralph Waldo Emerson with Annotations,* vol. 7, *1845–1848,* ed. Edward Waldo Emerson and Waldo Emerson Forbes (London: Constable, 1913), 206.

15. On occasion, Polk intervened to keep a slave family together or acted on similarly benign impulses. William Dusinberre, *Slavemaster President: The Double Career of James Polk* (New York: Oxford Univ. Press, 2003), 80–84. In his 1849 will, he stipulated that, if he should outlive his wife, upon his own death all of his

slaves would be emancipated. If his wife should outlive him, he left the decision in her hands but hoped that she would emancipate their slaves "if . . . she shall deem it proper." As events turned out, however, Sarah Polk outlived her husband by four decades, dying in 1891, rendering her husband's wishes irrelevant in that slavery in the United States had been abolished in 1865. Polk, will of 1849, in *Wills of the U.S. Presidents,* comp. Herbert R. Collins and David B. Weaver (New York: Communications Channels, 1976), 94. For Polk's attitudes toward slavery, see Dusinberre, *Slavemaster President,* 17–22, 77–78, 120–21, 147, 168–69.

16. For an example of action against anti-Catholic bigotry, see entries of Oct. 14, 1846, and July 29, 1847, in Polk, *Diary* 2:187–91, 3:103–5; and Polk's endorsement of Edmund C. Bittinger to Polk, June 21, 1847, calendared in Polk, *Correspondence* 12:504. Polk also had friendly relations with New York City's bishop—later archbishop—John J. Hughes, arguably the most influential Irish American of that day; see Hughes to Polk, Aug. 10, 1847, Polk Papers. For more on Polk and Catholic Irish Americans, see Angela F. Murphy, *American Slavery, Irish Freedom: Abolition, Immigrant Citizenship, and the Transatlantic Movement for Irish Repeal* (Baton Rouge: Louisiana State Univ. Press, 2010), 177, 190, 191.

17. Polk to Robert Campbell Jr., Jan. 23, 1847, Polk, *Correspondence* 12:56–57. Major John W. Childress was the younger brother of Sarah Childress Polk.

18. Jeremiah George Harris to Polk, June 27, 1847, Polk, *Correspondence* 12:392–94.

19. Entry of May 11, 1846, Polk, *Diary* 1:391–92.

20. John Charles Frémont, quoted in Chaffin, *Pathfinder,* 249.

21. Polk to William Davidson et al., May 21, 1847, Polk, *Correspondence* 12:276–77.

6. The Road to Fort Sumter

1. For Mackenzie–Santa Anna affair, see John H. Savage to Polk, Apr. 19, 1847, Polk, *Correspondence* 12:189–92. The 1986

Iran-Contra scandal erupted after reports became public that, earlier that year, officials of the Reagan administration, in an effort to free U.S. hostages in Lebanon, had, in defiance of a U.S. ban on weapons sales to Iran, sent weapons to that country and had used profits from the sale to provide financial assistance to an insurgency by "Contras" in Nicaragua, then ruled by a Marxist government. Through several legislative actions during the early 1980s, Congress had imposed a ban on assistance to the Contras. Following investigations into the affair by House and Senate committees, as well as an independent commission, several administration officials were prosecuted by a special prosecutor and convicted of violations of various federal laws. The scandal became a defining episode of Reagan's second term.

2. Entry of Mar. 5, 1849, Polk, *Diary* 4:375–76.

3. Daniel Webster to Citizens of Worcester County, Mass., Jan. 3, 1844, in Daniel Webster, *Writings and Speeches of Daniel Webster Hitherto Uncollected,* vol. 4, ed. Fletcher Webster (Boston: Little, Brown, 1903), 423. In Webster's reference to Sparta, he was quoting former U.S. Secretary of State (1834–41) John Forsyth.

4. Polk to Pillow, Apr. 14, 1847, Polk, *Correspondence* 12:178.

BIBLIOGRAPHY

Manuscript Collections

Bancroft, George. Papers. Division of Rare and Manuscript Collections, Cornell University Library, Ithaca, New York.

——. Papers. Manuscript and Archives Division, New York Public Library.

——. Papers. Massachusetts Historical Society, Boston.

Dallas, Mifflin George. "Diary, 1848-1849." Photocopy of original. Historical Society of Pennsylvania, Philadelphia.

Marcy, William L. Papers. Manuscript Division, Library of Congress, Washington, D.C.

Polk, James K. Papers. Manuscript Division, Library of Congress, Washington, D.C.

Schouler, James. Autograph Collection. Massachusetts Historical Society, Boston.

Published Primary Sources

Bancroft, George. "Polk, James Knox." In *Appletons' Cyclopædia of American Biography,* edited by James Grant Wilson and John Fiske, 5:50–56. New York: D. Appleton, 1888.

Benton, Thomas Hart. *Thirty Years' View; or, A History of the Working of the American Government for Thirty Years, from 1820 to 1850.* Vol. 2. New York: D. Appleton, 1883.

Chase, Lucien B. *History of the Polk Administration.* New York: John F. Trow, 1850.

Douglass, Frederick. *The Frederick Douglass Papers.* Ser. 1, *Speeches, Debates, and Interviews,* vol. 1. Edited by John W. Blassingame. New Haven, Conn.: Yale Univ. Press, 1979.

Emerson, Ralph Waldo. *Journals of Ralph Waldo Emerson with Annotations*. Vol. 7, *1845–1848*. Edited by Edward Waldo Emerson and Waldo Emerson Forbes. London: Constable, 1913.

Foote, H. S. *Eulogy upon the Life and Character of James K. Polk, Late President of the United States, Delivered at Washington City, July 9, 1849*. Washington, D.C.: Thomas Ritchie, 1849.

Frémont, John. "The Conquest of California." *Century Illustrated Magazine* 41 (Apr. 1891): 917–28.

Garrett, Samuel B. *An Oration on the Life, Character and Public Services of the Late President James K. Polk, Delivered at Lawrenceburg, Tennessee, October 8, 1849*. Lawrenceburg: "Middle Tennessean" Office, 1849.

Jenkins, John S. *The Life of James Knox Polk: Late President of the United States*. Auburn, N.Y.: James M. Alden, 1850.

Mangum, Willie Person. *Papers of Willie Person Mangum*. Vol. 4, *1844–1846*. Edited by Henry Thomas Shanks. Raleigh: North Carolina Department of Archives and History, 1955.

The Man Who Shot Liberty Valence. Directed by John Ford. 123 min. Paramount Pictures, Los Angeles, 1962.

O'Sullivan, John L. "Annexation." *United States Magazine and Democratic Review* 17 (July–Aug. 1845): 5–10.

Polk, James K. *Correspondence of James K. Polk: Volume XII, January–July 1847*. Edited by Tom Chaffin and Michael David Cohen. Knoxville: Univ. of Tennessee Press, 2013.

———.*Correspondence of James K. Polk: Volume XI, 1846*. Edited by Wayne Cutler. Knoxville: Univ. of Tennessee Press, 2009.

———. *The Diary of James K. Polk during His Presidency, 1845 to 1849*. 4 vols. Edited by Milo Milton Quaife. Chicago: A. C. McClurg, 1910.

Richardson, James D., ed. *A Compilation of the Messages and Papers of the Presidents, 1789–1897*. Vol. 4. Washington, D.C.: GPO, 1897.

———. *A Compilation of the Messages and Papers of the Presidents, 1789–1897*. Vol. 9. Washington, D.C.: GPO, 1899.

Roosevelt, Theodore. *Life of Thomas Hart Benton.* Boston: Houghton Mifflin, 1886.

They Might Be Giants. "James K. Polk." Elektra Records, 1996.

Thoreau, Henry David. *Henry David Thoreau: Collected Essays and Poems.* Edited by Elizabeth Hall Witherell. New York: Library of America, 2001.

Truman, Harry S. *Affection and Trust: The Personal Correspondence of Harry S. Truman and Dean Acheson, 1953–1971.* Edited by Ray Geselbracht. New York: Alfred A. Knopf, 2010.

———. *Truman Speaks.* New York: Columbia Univ. Press, 1960.

Webster, Daniel. *Writings and Speeches of Daniel Webster Hitherto Uncollected.* Vol. 4. Edited by Fletcher Webster. Boston: Little, Brown, 1903.

Whitman, Walt. *Walt Whitman: Complete Poetry and Collected Prose.* Edited by Justin Kaplan. New York: Library of America, 1982.

Wills of the U.S. Presidents. Compiled by Herbert R. Collins and David B. Weaver. New York: Communications Channels, 1976.

Woodbury, Levi. *Eulogy on the Life, Character, and Public Services of the Late Ex-President Polk: Delivered at the Request of the Municipal Authorities of the City of Boston, July 25, 1849.* Boston: J. H. Eastburn, 1849.

Secondary Sources

Bauer, K. Jack. *The Mexican War, 1846–1848.* New York: Macmillan, 1974.

Bergeron, Paul H. *The Presidency of James K. Polk.* Lawrence: Univ. Press of Kansas, 1987.

Borneman, Walter R. *Polk: The Man Who Transformed the Presidency and America.* New York: Random House, 2008.

Byrnes, Mark E. *James K. Polk: A Biographical Companion.* Santa Barbara, Calif.: ABC-CLIO, 2001.

Chaffin, Tom. *Fatal Glory: Narciso López and the First Clandestine U.S. War against Cuba.* Charlottesville: Univ. Press of Virginia, 1996. Reprint, Baton Rouge: Louisiana State Univ. Press, 2003.

———. "Mitt Romney: The Second Coming of James K. Polk?" *Atlantic.com,* Oct. 3, 2012. http://www.theatlantic.com/politics/archive/2012/10/mitt-romney-the-second-coming-of-james-k-polk/263018/.

———. *Pathfinder: John Charles Frémont and the Course of American Empire.* New York: Hill & Wang, 2002.

Conlin, Joseph R. *The American Past: A Survey of American History.* Vol. 1, *To 1877.* 3rd ed. Boston: Wadsworth, Cengage Learning, 2012.

del Olmo, Frank. "Line Drawn in 1848 Shaped Who We Are." *Los Angeles Times,* March 1, 1998.

Dusinberre, William. *Slavemaster President: The Double Career of James Polk.* New York: Oxford Univ. Press, 2003.

Foner, Eric. *Politics and Ideology in the Age of the Civil War.* New York: Oxford Univ. Press, 1981.

Garrison, George Pierce. *Westward Extension, 1841–1850.* New York: Harper & Brothers, 1906.

Gash, Norman. *Sir Robert Peel: The Life of Sir Robert Peel after 1830.* London: Longman, 1972.

Graebner, Norman A. *Empire on the Pacific: A Study in Continental Expansion.* Claremont, Calif.: Regina Books, 1983.

Greenberg, Amy S. *A Wicked War: Polk, Clay, Lincoln and the 1846 U.S. Invasion of Mexico.* New York: Alfred A. Knopf, 2012.

Handlin, Lilian. *George Bancroft: The Intellectual as Democrat.* New York: Harper & Row, 1984.

Harlow, Neal. *California Conquered: The Annexation of a Mexican Province, 1846–1850.* Berkeley and Los Angeles: Univ. of California Press, 1982.

Horsman, Reginald. *Race and Manifest Destiny: Origins of American Racial Anglo-Saxonism.* Cambridge: Harvard Univ. Press, 1981.

Kaplan, Robert D. *The Revenge of Geography: What the Map Tells Us About Coming Conflicts and the Battle Against Fate*. New York: Random House, 2012.

Krainik, Clifford. "A 'Dark Horse' in Sunlight and Shadow: Daguerreotypes of President James K. Polk," *White House History* 2, no. 1 (June 1997): 38–49.

Leonard, Thomas M. *James Polk: A Clear and Unquestionable Destiny*. Biographies in American Foreign Policy series. Lanham, Md.: Rowman & Littlefield, 2000.

Luff, John Nicholas. *The Postage Stamps of the United States*. N.Y: Scott Stamp and Coin Co., 1902.

Mailer, Norman. *Conversations with Norman Mailer*. Edited by J. Michael Lennon. Oxford: Univ. Press of Mississippi, 2008.

———. *Marilyn*. New York: Grosset & Dunlap, 1973.

May, Robert E. *Manifest Destiny's Underworld: Filibustering in Antebellum America*. Chapel Hill: Univ. of North Carolina Press, 2001.

McCormac, Eugene Irving. *James K. Polk: A Political Biography*. Berkeley and Los Angeles: Univ. of California Press, 1922.

McDonough, John. "History of the Collection." In *James K. Polk Papers: A Finding Aid to the Collection in the Library of Congress*. Rev. ed. Washington, D.C.: Manuscript Division, Library of Congress, 2010.

Merk, Frederick. *Manifest Destiny and Mission in American History*. 1963. Reprint, Cambridge: Harvard Univ. Press, 1995.

Merry, Robert W. *A Country of Vast Designs: James K. Polk, the Mexican War and the Conquest of the American Continent*. New York: Simon & Schuster, 2009.

Montville, Leigh. *The Big Bam: The Life and Times of Babe Ruth*. New York: Random House, 2007.

Morrison, Michael A. *Slavery and the American West: The Eclipse of Manifest Destiny*. Chapel Hill: Univ. of North Carolina Press, 1999.

Murphy, Angela F. *American Slavery, Irish Freedom: Abolition, Immigrant Citizenship, and the Transatlantic Movement for Irish Repeal.* Baton Rouge: Louisiana State Univ. Press, 2010.

Nobles, Gregory H. *American Frontiers: Cultural Encounters and Continental Conquest.* New York: Hill and Wang, 1997.

Nugent, Walter. *Habits of Empire: A History of American Expansion.* New York: Alfred Knopf, 2008.

Nye, Russel B. *George Bancroft: Brahmin Rebel.* New York: Alfred K. Knopf, 1945.

Onuf, Peter S. *Jefferson's Empire: The Language of American Nationhood.* Charlottesville: Univ. Press of Virginia, 2000.

Pinheiro, John C. *Manifest Ambition: James K. Polk and Civil-Military Relations during the Mexican War.* Westport, Conn.: Praeger Security International, 2007.

Pletcher, David M. *The Diplomacy of Annexation: Texas, Oregon, and the Mexican War.* Columbia: Univ. of Missouri Press, 1973.

Ritchie, Donald. *Press Gallery: Congress and the Washington Correspondents.* Cambridge, Mass: Harvard Univ. Press, 1993.

Ronda, James P. *Lewis & Clark among the Indians.* Lincoln: University of Nebraska Press, 1984.

Sampson, Robert D. *John L. O'Sullivan and His Times.* Kent, Ohio: Kent State Univ. Press, 2003.

Schlesinger, Arthur M. "Historians Rate the U.S. Presidents." *Life,* Nov. 1, 1948, 65–66.

———. "Our Presidents: A Rating by 75 Historians." *New York Times Magazine,* July 29, 1962, 12, 40, 41, 43.

Schlesinger, Arthur M., Jr. "Rating the Presidents: Washington to Clinton." *Political Science Quarterly* 112 (Summer 1997): 179–90.

Schouler, James. *History of the United States of America, under the Constitution.* Vol. 4, *1831–1847.* Washington, D.C.: William H. Morrison, 1889.

Seigenthaler, John. *James K. Polk.* American Presidents series. New York: Times Books, 2003.

Sellers, Charles. *James K. Polk: Continentalist, 1843–1846.* Princeton, N.J.: Princeton Univ. Press, 1966.

———. *James K. Polk: Jacksonian, 1795–1843.* Princeton, N.J.: Princeton Univ. Press, 1957.

Sexton, Jay. *The Monroe Doctrine: Empire and Nation in Nineteenth-Century America.* New York: Hill & Wang, 2011.

Stephanson, Anders. *Manifest Destiny: American Expansion and the Empire of Right.* New York: Hill & Wang, 1995.

Tindall, George Brown, with David E. Shi. *America: A Narrative History.* 3rd ed. New York: W. W. Norton, 1984.

Turner, Frederick Jackson. "The Significance of the Frontier in American History." *Proceedings of the State Historical Society of Wisconsin* 41 (1894): 79–112.

Van Alstyne, Richard W. *The Rising American Empire.* 1960. Reprint, New York: W. W. Norton, 1974.

Ward, Jon. "The One-Termer?" *Huffington Post,* Aug. 21, 2012. http://www.huffingtonpost.com/2012/08/21/the-one-termer_n_1819608.html/.

Weber, David J. *The Mexican Frontier, 1821–1846: The American Southwest under Mexico.* Albuquerque: Univ. of New Mexico Press, 1982.

Weinberg, Albert K. *Manifest Destiny: A Study of Nationalist Expansionism in American History.* Baltimore: Johns Hopkins Press, 1935.

Winders, Richard Bruce. *Mr. Polk's Army: The American Military Experience in the Mexican War.* College Station: Texas A&M Univ. Press, 1997.

INDEX